C PROGRAMMING GUIDELINES

Second Edition

Thomas Plum

Plum Hall Inc
1 Spruce Avenue
Cardiff New Jersey 08232

Library of Congress Cataloging-in-Publication Data

Plum,Thomas, 1943-
      C programming guidelines / Thomas Plum. -- 2nd ed.
         p.   cm.
      Bibliography: p.
      Includes index.
      ISBN 0-911537-07-4 : $30.00
      1. C (Computer program language)   I. Title.
   QA76.73.C15P57 1989
   005.13'3--dc20   89-15992
                                             CIP

        Acknowledgement of trademarks: UNIX is a trademark of AT&T Bell Laboratories;
PDP-11 and VAX are trademarks of Digital Equipment Corporation; Xenix and MS-DOS
are trademarks of Microsoft Corporation; IDRIS is a trademark of Itermetrics Corporation;
Tplus is a trademark of Textware International; Safe C is a trademark of Catalytix Corporation; POSIX is a trademark of the IEEE; MC68000 is a trademark of Motorola Inc. C
is not a trademark, nor are the names of the software development commands such as cc.

ISBN 0-911537-07-4

10 9 8 7 6 5 4 3 2 1

For Joan

PREFACE TO THE SECOND EDITION

Why do programming projects adopt coding standards for C? There are three primary reasons:

Reliability: Each program should produce a predictable, correct behavior.

Readability/Maintainability: Clarity and consistency assist maintainers in making revisions properly.

Portability: Nowadays, people expect to be able to move applications to new hardware and new compilers.

The prospects for portable C have been greatly enhanced by the development of an official standard for C. As of mid-1989, the ANSI committee X3J11 has nearly completed the standardization of C. While the formally-adopted standard is not expected until the latter part of 1989, many vendors are already implementing most of the ideas of the X3J11 draft. Furthermore, the draft itself has changed very little at the most recent X3J11 meetings. It seems, therefore, an appropriate time to revise the Plum Hall guidelines to take account of the recent evolution of C.

If your compilers are all from the pre-Standard generation, and you expect to keep using them for the next year, the first edition of these guidelines is still appropriate. Most compilers, however, already incorporate ideas of the new Standard, and will be fully Standard within a year.

What guidelines will ensure the most reliable and portable usage of Standard C compilers?

Some answers to this question are elaborated at length in the Plum Hall book *Learning to Program in C (Second Edition)*. This book introduces project-oriented C using Standard C throughout. Further details are found in *Reliable Data Structures in C*. That book also introduced several suggestions for improving the reliability of C programs in general. In these guidelines, whenever a rule is relevant to a section from *Reliable Data Structures in C*, a notation such as (RDS 2.3) will appear, indicating a reference to section 2.3.

A few of the new guidelines are derived from another Plum Hall book, *Efficient C*, indicated as "EFC". (We have adopted the typographical convention of putting punctuation inside quotation marks only if the punctuation is part of the quoted material.)

Some of the names and definitions in earlier Plum Hall books have been changed. *RDS* referred to "unsafe" macros that should not have side effects in their arguments; these Guidelines use the term "unprotected" to avoid any confusion with issues of product "safety" as commonly understood. (See Section 4.14_macros.) And the defined-type scheme for portable data has been simplified, in large part due to the greater uniformity of Standard C compilers. (See Section 1.3_stdtypes.)

Plum Hall also provides these Guidelines in machine-readable form for projects wishing to incorporate this material into their local programming standard.

In addition to the people who generously assisted with the first edition, several other people have provided thoughtful comments. My thanks to Phil Housley, P. J. Plauger, Roland Racko, Russ Schnall, Christopher Skelly, Henry Tieding, Frank Vretos, and Ed Wells.

Thomas Plum

PREFACE TO THE FIRST EDITION

C is a highly portable language which generates efficient code for a wide variety of modern computers. It was originally implemented on the UNIX operating system for the DEC PDP-11 by Dennis Ritchie. Within Bell Laboratories it is widely used for systems and application programming. In the years since it was made available to universities and commercial organizations, it has proved valuable for systems programming, switching and communications, microprocessors, text processing, process control, test equipment, and the creation of numerous application packages. Its audience has been widened by compilers for many operating systems besides UNIX; these compilers have been produced by numerous software companies, among which the pioneer was Whitesmiths, Ltd. Whitesmiths' IDRIS operating system (on which this book was composed) is, like UNIX, almost entirely written in C.

Programming standards can be valuable to any organization producing programs in C. Its compact notation and absence of restrictions can be used in an undisciplined fashion to produce programs unreadable to any but the original author — if indeed the author can read them after the passage of time! A uniformity of style can make the thankless task of the maintainer much easier. The code can be modified much easier when standards are followed.

In addition to aiding consistency, standards also enhance portability of the source code, since one of the important virtues of the C language is its combination of portability and efficiency.

However, achieving portability requires attention to a small set of problem areas, which are addressed by the portability standards in this book.

Disagreements over programming style have been a primary obstacle to teams attempting to work closely together. One suggestion for preventing style arguments is for each project to choose its own standard in the early phases of the project. The layout of this book was chosen to facilitate its use in a pick-and-choose fashion. Space has been left for local notes so that the book could be used to keep a record of meetings regarding style agreements. Each section is named (in the style of UNIX manuals) as well as numbered, for ease of later reference.

The author asks in accordance with copyright laws that this book not be run through the copying machine; Plum Hall Inc will make available on a reasonable license arrangement both hard-copy and machine-readable originals for projects that wish to incorporate this material in their own standard.

In this edition of *C Programming Guidelines*, the usage of types, function names, and indentation conforms to the format of the UNIX manuals published by Bell Laboratories. The style usage is consistent with *Learning to Program in C*, by Thomas Plum (Plum Hall Inc, 1983).

Previous editions of these guidelines made reference to the (now obsolescent) UNIX Version 6 compiler. Such references are omitted from this edition. Where portability is a concern, do not use the V6 compiler.

This book is also available in the format of the manuals from Whitesmiths, Ltd., in *C Programming Standards and Guidelines: Version W (Whitesmiths). [Now out of print, as of 1988.]* The discussions of portability, however, apply to both systems.

During 1983, a committee was formed by the American National Standards Institute (ANSI) to standardize the definition of the C language. Previous editions of this book had the word "standards" in the title. To avoid any possible confusion with the development of the ANSI standard, I have dropped the word "standard" from the title of this book. I thank the other members of the ANSI X3J11 committee for enlightening discussions about the C language. In my opinion, based on information currently available, programs written according to the guidelines in this book should be well prepared for the eventual ANSI standard; however, no one can give any official guarantees as of this date.

For thoughtful comments and suggestions on various drafts of this material, I am indebted to Tom Bishop, Debbie Fullam, David Graham, Joan Hall, Brian Kernighan, Bill Koenig, Mark Krieger, Eli Lamb, Ian MacLeod, Bill Masek, Paul Matthews, P. J. Plauger, Ed Rathje, Chaim Schaap, and Steve Schustack.

And for their steadfast support, my heartfelt thanks to Suzanne Battista, Linda Deutsch, Anne Hall, Joan Hall, Karl Karlstrom, and Sonya Whynman.

Thomas Plum

CONTENTS

NAME
0.1_standards - standards and guidelines

STANDARD
Criteria labeled as "STANDARD" are mandatory for all code included in a product.

The need for exceptions may occasionally arise, but the exception requires a specific justification, and the justification should be documented with the source code. This is a "permissive" approach to exceptions; this book is not intended to satisfy any legal, auditing, or quality-assurance criteria.

Project-wide exceptions to the standards may be justified and should be documented as an appendix to the standard.

Criteria labeled as "GUIDELINE" are recommended practices. Experience has shown that differing approaches can coexist in these areas. It is expected that, in general, a majority of programmers will follow the guidelines, so that they represent a widely-accepted pattern.

NAME
   1.1_lexdata - lexical rules for variables

STANDARD
   Names of variables and functions should be written all in lower
   case. Use 31-character limits for all names, internal and external.
   When porting to "deficient" environments in which linkers impose
   short name limits upon external symbols, each package's header file
   can #define long names into unique short names:

```
#include "portdefs.h"  /* described in CPG 4.19_headers */
#if NAM_LEN_EXTERNAL < 12
    #define data_base_update datab1
#endif
```

   All names should be explicitly declared. Within each function, first
   come any register variable names (ordered by importance), and then
   the other names.

   External names beginning with underscore should be reserved for
   the compiler or other systems programs, and should not be used in
   project code.

   Declarations should be written with only one variable per source
   line; however, when several uninitialized variables share the same
   type and properties, they may share a one-line declaration. Whenever a comment can add information, use it.

   Initializers of structures, unions, and arrays should be formatted
   with braces around each sub-aggregate, one row per line:

```
static short x[2][5] =
    {
    {1, 2, 3, 4, 5},
    {6, 7, 8, 9, 10},
    };
```

   Standard C allows automatic aggregates to be initialized, following
   the same "constant-expression" rules as for static aggregates.

   Variable name and type should be separated by single spaces, and
   descriptive comments should be attached at a lined-up tab position:

```
bool canhit;          /* can player's hand take hit? */
short tophand;        /* how many hands is player playing : {1:2} */
```

   To accomodate the widest variety of compilers and linkers, each
   file-level declaration should be either a "definition" (without the
   keyword extern, and with an initializer) or a "reference-declaration"
   (or "ref-declaration", with the keyword extern, and no initializer).

14   Copyright © Plum Hall Inc 1989

Storage class (if any) should precede the type specifier. (RDS 3.1)

JUSTIFICATION

The rules pinpoint the location of declarations, avoid conflicts of upper- and lower-case names, and encourage documentation of the meaning of variable names.

Standard C allows for linkers which insist on exactly one "definition" for each external variable. Some environments (e.g., UNIX) are more permissive, but if the stricter rules are observed, these environments will diagnose any instances which are non-portable to the more restrictive environments.

The `register` variables are ordered for purposes of portable efficiency — compilers differ in the number of `register` requests honored.

ALTERNATIVES

Some projects prefer only one space between type and variable name, with comments attached with at least one tab:

```
bool mpflg = NO;     /* preprocessed macros flag */
bool ff;     /* fork flag */
```

Alternatives such as this one, which avoid columnar layout of source code, should be adopted only when convenient full-screen editing is unavailable.

On the other hand, some projects prefer an even stricter layout: never more than one declaration per line, always commented.

A "common" declaration is an external declaration containing neither the keyword `extern` nor an initializer. Some environments such as UNIX allow the more permissive "common" model of linkage, in which any number of "common" declarations will all be linked together. Code which is intended only for such environments can therefore follow the more permissive "common" model.

[LOCAL NOTES]

NAME
   1.2_names - choosing variable names

GUIDELINE
   Names should be chosen to be meaningful; their meaning should be
   exact and should be preserved throughout the program.

   For example, variables which count something should be initialized
   to the count which is valid at that point; i.e., if the count is initially
   zero, the variable should be initialized to 0, not to -1 or some other
   number.

   This means that each variable has an *invariant* (i.e. unchanging)
   meaning — a property that is true throughout the program. The
   readability of the code is enhanced by *minimizing the "domains of
   exceptions"*, which are the regions of the program in which the
   invariant property fails. For example, in this short loop, the variable nc has the invariant property of being equal to the number of
   characters read so far. The only exception to the property is during the time between reading a character and incrementing the
   counter:

```
short nc;    /* number of characters */

nc = 0;
while (getchar() != EOF)
    ++nc;
```

   Abbreviations for meaningful names should be chosen by a uniform scheme. For example, use the leading consonant of each word
   in a name.

   Abbreviations should not form letter combinations that suggest
   unintended meanings; the name inch is a misleading abbreviation
   for "input character". Similarly, names should not create misleading phonemes; the name metach (abbreviation for "meta-character")
   forms the phonemes "me-tach" in English, obscuring the meaning.

   Names should not be re-defined in inner blocks.

   A special case of meaningful names is the use of standard short
   names like c for characters, i, j, k for indexes, n for counters, p or
   q for pointers, s for strings, and x, y, z for (floating-point)
   mathematical variables.

   In separate functions, variables with identical meanings can have
   the same name. But when the meanings are only similar or coin-
   cidental, use different names.

16

Names over four characters in length should differ by at least two characters:

```
systst, sysstst /* bad - easily confused */
```

The following abbreviations can be used within comments for greater precision (RDS 0.1):

```
nul                means the char value '\0'
a[i:j]             means the subarray a[i] through a[j]
a[*]               means the entire array a (for emphasis)
p[*]               means the entire array accessed through p
a[*] => sorted  means that a[*] is now sorted
```

Include "one-too-far" values in the ranges for variables, if they are needed for loop terminations or other testing purposes. (RDS 2.6)

Document the defining properties of declared names in a comment on the declaration. To encourage use of such comments, and to create the potential for future automation of property-checking, use a concise convention such as "space, colon, space, property name". (RDS 2.9, slightly revised) Example:

```
int hand;   /* which hand : {1:2} */
```

Choose project-wide consistent names for the important properties of data, and use these names in the documenting comments. Examples from *LPC*:

```
{lo:hi}         means the range from lo to hi .

{>lo:<hi}       means the range of values greater than lo and less
                than hi.
{lo, b:c, hi}   means the range of values lo, b through c, and hi.

bits(n)         used for bitwise operations on n bits.

bool            tested for either false (zero) or true (non-zero).

metachar        the range {EOF, 0:UCHAR_MAX} for the returned value from
                functions such as  getchar .
string          contains a null-terminator (for array of chars, or
                array of chars designated by a pointer).
dollars         represents currency in dollars; i.e. the value 12.34
                means 12 dollars and 34 cents.
pennies         represents currency in pennies; i.e. the value 12.34
                means 12 and 34/100 cents.
```

The dollars and pennies properties illustrate the use of "property comments" for units of measure; other instances might be meters, grams, seconds, etc. Always indicate units of measure whenever appropriate.

17

Ensure that the defining properties remain invariant (unchanging) as much as possible throughout the computation, and document any exceptions. (RDS 3.1)

Do not use the same variable for different purposes.

An array is *complete* if none of its elements are in an undefined (uninitialized or "garbage") state. A program is easier to write correctly and to understand if all arrays are made complete before the array is used. (RDS 3.1)

If an array's defining property can be true even if some elements are in an undefined state, indicate the property on the array's declaration. For example,

```
char message[10];      /* : string */
```

(RDS 3.1)

Use executable assertions whenever they are simpler than the code being protected, and when the time to execute the assertions is not much greater than the time required to execute the code. (See 6.7_assert, and RDS 3.2.)

A structure is *well-defined* if the values of all its members have whatever defining properties were specified in comments. Thus, for example, if a member is specified to have a range of values like (0:9), that member must have a value between 0 and 9 in order for the structure to be considered well-defined.

For structures, the rule of "minimizing the domains of exceptions" means that members should be individually well-defined and in a consistent relationship to each other.

If a structure is not well-defined when initialized to zero, document this fact in a comment. (The program will in general be simpler if the members are defined such that the zero-initialized structure is well-defined.) (RDS 6.3)

JUSTIFICATION

Readability of the code is greatly enhanced by the reader's ability to construct natural assertions about the meaning of names anywhere they appear in the code, and about the specific properties of the data.

[LOCAL NOTES]

[LOCAL NOTES]

NAME
    1.3_stdtypes - standard defined-types

STANDARD
    Programs should use a project-wide standard set of data-type names.

    The set of standard types presented here are a mixture of standard C types (sometimes with usage restrictions) and defined-types defined by the header portdefs.h. (All the headers described in these guidelines are described in detail in Section 4.19_headers.)

    There are three purposes for this usage of types: portability to the widest range of machines and compilers, semantic clarity regarding the usage of the data, and brevity.

```
char       - an 8+ bit item used only for characters and memory bytes

schar      - an 8+ bit signed integer (signed char)
short      - a 16+ bit signed integer (short int)
long       - a 32+ bit signed integer (long int)

uchar      - an 8+ bit unsigned integer (unsigned char)
ushort     - a 16+ bit unsigned integer (unsigned short)
ulong      - a 32+ bit unsigned integer (unsigned long)

float      - single precision floating point number
double     - double precision floating point number
ldouble    - long double precision floating point number (long double)

bool       - int (or smaller), tested only for zero or non-zero
metachar   - short (or int), for the range {EOF, 0:UCHAR_MAX}
int        - for function parameters, returned values and registers
uint       - unsigned int (parameters, returned values and registers)

size_t     - an unsigned integer, for holding the size of an object
```

    Avoid careless dependence on the int size of the computer. This is especially important on machines where int and long are the same size; careless code will not port correctly to smaller machines.

    There are, however, three uses of the int (or uint) type which are appropriate for portable programs. First of all, a function's returned value may be written as int. (Many existing library functions are defined to have int returned values.) The second portable usage of int is for function parameters, again for consistency with standard libraries. The third usage of int is for register integer variables. In all these usages, programs should assume that int contains at least 16 bits and perhaps more.

Most of these defined-types are created at the choice of the project, but one of them is defined in several Standard headers: size_t is the proper type for holding the sizeof any object. It is the proper type for the storage size passed to allocation functions such as calloc. Up until recently, an unsigned int was adequate for this purpose, but in some environments an unsigned long is required.

For maximum portability, programs should not make assumptions about the size of pointer-to-function.

Programs must use the semantically correct data-type name, even where several similar names map onto the same raw C language type.

Bitwise operations should be performed upon unsigned data, for maximum portability.

ALTERNATIVES

The first edition described more defined-types, for portability to then-existing compilers. Usage of the following types may be continued for compatibility:

```
tiny      - an 8+ bit integer used for a quantity
tbits     - an 8+ bit integer used for bit manipulation
tbool     - an 8+ bit integer, but only tested against zero
utiny     - an 8+ bit unsigned integer used for a quantity
bits      - a 16+ bit integer used for bit manipulation
lbits     - a 32+ bit integer used for bit manipulation
data_ptr  - a pointer adequate for any pointer to data (synonym for void *)
```

[LOCAL NOTES]

NAME
    1.4_constants - maintainability of constants

STANDARD
    Any constant which might change during revision or modification
    should be "manifest" ("clearly apparent to the sight or understand-
    ing; obvious"). Specifically, it should be given an upper-case name
    (via #define or enum).

    If it is only used in one file, it should be defined at the head of
    that file; if used in multiple files, it should be defined in a header.

    Standard manifest constants should be used where appropriate.
    Examples from <stdio.h>:

```
BUFSIZ      the size of a standard file buffer
NULL        zero, as a pointer value
EOF         the end-of-file return value from getchar
SEEK_SET    seek relative to file start
SEEK_CUR    seek relative to current position
SEEK_END    seek relative to file end
```

    Always terminate successful execution with

```
exit(0);
```

    In strictly portable programs, unsuccessful execution should be ter-
    minated using the manifest constant EXIT_FAILURE from <stdlib.h>:

```
exit(EXIT_FAILURE);
```

    Other useful manifest constants should be provided by a local stan-
    dard header file (see 4.19_headers). For example,

```
TRUE    1   boolean
FALSE   0   boolean
YES     1   same as TRUE
NO      0   same as FALSE
STDIN   0   (low-level I/O) file descriptor for standard input
STDOUT  1   (low-level I/O) file descriptor for standard output
STDERR  2   (low-level I/O) file descriptor for standard error output
```

    If there are limitations on the modifiability of a defined constant,
    indicate the limitations with a comment:

```
#define EOF (-1)  /* DO NOT MODIFY: ctype.h expects -1 */
```

    (RDS 1.1)

    If one definition affects another, embody the relationship in the
    definition; do not give two independent definitions. (RDS 1.1)

If a value is given for a defined name, do not defeat its modifiability by assuming its value in expressions. (RDS 1.1)

When defining manifest constants for array bounds and subscript limits, use the number of elements rather than the index of the last element (in zero-origin C, these differ by one).

Write programs as if enumeration variables could receive no values other than the associated enumeration constants.

JUSTIFICATION

Constants that are hard-coded (otherwise known as "magic numbers" because they mysteriously appear with no explanation) are hard to locate when modifying the program. Furthermore, instances of "constant minus one" or "constant plus one" are even more elusive to the maintenance programmer.

EXAMPLE

```
if (index < 100)    /* bad - no explanation, hard to modify */

#define SIZE 100
   ...
if (index < SIZE)   /* good */
```

[LOCAL NOTES]

NAME
   1.5_wordlen - word and byte size

STANDARD
   C programs should assume the following sizes for data:

```
char     8 bits (or more)

short    16 bits (or more)

long     32 bits (or more)
```

The following rule is necessary for porting to the widest variety of target machines and compilers: A program should never rely on data size (or casts) to truncate expressions to a specific number of bits. Use masks (bit-and) to produce a specific number of bits.

If, alternatively, the project has determined that all future targets will be 8-16-32 environments, such restrictions are not necessary. But then this limitation should be clearly stated in project specifications or atop source files, headers, etc.

Bitwise constants can be made more portable by relying on the "bit-not" operator to set high-order one-bits. For example, to turn off the low-order bit of a variable b:

```
b &= ~1;        /* good */

b &= 0177776;   /* bad - turns off high bits */
                /*       on 32-bit machine    */
```

JUSTIFICATION
   The object of this standard is portability. There are C compilers with char's of 8, 9, or 10 bits, with short's of 16, 18, 20, and 36 bits, and with long's of 32, 36, and 40 bits. And even within the eight-bit world, bitwise constants are subject to the uncertainty of the int size.

24

[LOCAL NOTES]

NAME
    1.6_byteorder - byte ordering

STANDARD
    Portability demands that programs not depend upon the order of
    bytes within an integral or floating number. For example, on
    machines such as PDP-11, the low-order byte of a short integer is
    stored in memory before the high-order byte; but on other
    machines such as MC68000, the high-order byte is stored first.

    In portable code, question each appearance of a pointer cast:

```
        char *p;
        short n;

        p = (char *)&n; /* bad - non-portable, machine-dependent byte */
```

    Binary data written on one machine will be portable to another
    machine only if byte-ordering dependencies are eliminated. A
    canonical ordering for binary data must be chosen. Before writing
    binary data, it should be converted to this canonical order; after
    reading canonical binary data, it should be converted back. The
    same considerations apply to floating data.

JUSTIFICATION
    It is possible to write C programs which will give identical results
    on machines with different byte-orders, but one must follow the
    rules given above.

[LOCAL NOTES]

[LOCAL NOTES]

NAME
1.7_charconsts - character constants

STANDARD
Portability requires that character constants not contain more than one character. The differences in machine byte-order may cause multi-character constants to differ either in numeric value or in character sequence.

EXAMPLE

```
short crlf = '\r\n';    /* bad - uses char constant */
```

If the characters are simply being used as a string value, use a proper C string:

```
char crlf[] = "\r\n";    /* good - uses string constant */
```

Often, multi-character constants are introduced in order to make a single integer value from two or more char's for example to switch on the value. In such cases, there is a portable means to achieve the same efficiency:

```
#define CHAR2(a, b)  (((a) << CHAR_BIT) + (b))
...
switch (CHAR2(c1, c2))
    {
case CHAR2('e', 'd'):
    /* ... */
```

JUSTIFICATION
The multi-character constants are intrinsically non-portable.

[LOCAL NOTES]

[LOCAL NOTES]

NAME
    1.8_ptrtypes - pointer types

STANDARD
    Pointers which will point to several different types of object should
    be declared as void * generic pointers.

    Pointers-to-functions should be given typedef'ed types, to improve
    the conceptual clarity:

```
/* an INT_F_INT is a pointer to function of int arg returning int */
typedef int (*INT_F_INT)(int);

INT_F_INT pfa;   /* a pointer whose type is INT_F_INT */
```

    In some environments, pointers-to-data and pointers-to-function
    have different sizes and representations. The void * generic
    pointers should contain only addresses of data, and not of func-
    tions. In particular, the symbol NULL should not be used with
    pointers-to-functions. A simple integer constant zero will suffice
    for the occasional "null pointer-to-function", as in

```
int func(
    INT_F_INT pfa)  /* one pointer argument */
    {
    if (pfa == 0)
        /* handle the null-pointer case  ... */
    /* ... */
```

[LOCAL NOTES]

[LOCAL NOTES]

NAME
    1.9_ptrconv - pointer conversions

STANDARD
    Programs should contain no pointer conversions, except for the fol-
    lowing safe ones:

    NULL may be assigned to any pointer-to-data.

    Allocation functions (e.g. malloc) will guarantee safe align-
    ment, and return a void * generic pointer, so the returned
    value may be assigned to any pointer-to-data. Use sizeof to
    specify the amount of storage to be allocated.

    Pointers to an object of a given size may be converted to a
    pointer-to-character or a generic pointer and back again,
    without change. For example, a pointer-to-long may be
    assigned to a pointer-to-character variable which is later
    assigned back to a pointer-to-long. Any use of the intermedi-
    ate pointer, other than equality-tests or assigning it back to
    the original type, gives machine-dependent code.

    Integers (properly cast) may be assigned to pointers, or pointers
    (properly cast) to integers, but *only* in non-portable hardware-
    dependent functions, such as device drivers.

JUSTIFICATION
    Other conversions will be compiler-dependent or machine-
    dependent, or both.

EXAMPLE

```
        short *pi;
        char *pc;

        pi = NULL;  /* ok to assign NULL */

        pi = malloc(sizeof(short));
                    /* ok to assign malloc() */

        pc = pi;    /* ok to assign to char pointer */
        pi = pc;    /* and then assign back to larger-type */

        /* Non-portable (e.g., device driver) examples ... */
        ioport = (short *)0xA220;      /* hardware-dependent I/O port address */
        offset = (int)buf_addr & 0x1FF; /* hardware-dependent bit manipulation */
```

[LOCAL NOTES]

NAME
    1.10_alloc - allocation integrity

STANDARD

A function in which the address of an automatic variable is assigned to a non-automatic pointer must contain a comment to that effect. In any function with such a comment, each return from the function is an event requiring verification that no dangling pointers are left. (RDS 4.3)

When a pointer p is passed to the free function, the programmer must determine how many pointers are pointing into the freed storage. (This number is known as the "reference count" of the storage.) Steps must be taken (such as assigning NULL) to ensure that none of these pointers are subsequently used to access the freed storage. For example, the local.h header can define a macro:

```
#define FREE(p)  (free(p), p = NULL)
```
(RDS 7.1)

For every instance in which a program allocates storage, there should be an easily identifiable instance in which that storage is later freed. (RDS 7.1)

For every instance of fopen, there should be an easily identifiable instance of fclose (and perhaps an ferror test too — see 5.5_defensive).

[LOCAL NOTES]

[LOCAL NOTES]

NAME
1.11_structs - structures

STANDARD

In portable programming, do not hard-code the numeric values of structure offsets. The values may be different in each environment. Refer to members by their symbolic member names only. (RDS 6.1) If the numeric offset of a structure member is needed, use the macro offsetof from <stddef.h>.

Tag and member names with leading underscore should only appear in code that is privy to the internal details of the associated data structure, not in "user-level" portable code. (RDS 6.2)

Use the "leading underscore" name format for tag and member names if the internal details of the structure are not to be inspected by functions outside of the package. Conversely, avoid leading underscores if the details of the structure are available for inspection by functions that use the structure. (RDS 6.2)

In portable code, do not depend upon the allocation order of bit-fields within a word. Do not depend upon having more than 16 bits per word. (RDS 6.5)

[LOCAL NOTES]

[LOCAL NOTES]

NAME

1.12_strings - string literals

STANDARD

String literals should not be modified. To achieve a modifiable string, use a named array of characters.

In other words, if mktemp is a function that modifies its string argument, do not write

```
mktemp("/tmp/edXXXXXX");
```

Instead, use a named array:

```
static char fname[] = "/tmp/edXXXXXX";

mktemp(fname);
```

[LOCAL NOTES]

[LOCAL NOTES]

NAME
2.1_lexops - lexical rules for operators

STANDARD
The primary operators "arrow" (->), "dot" (.), and "subscript" ([]) should be written with no space around them:

```
p->m   s.m   a[i]
```

Parentheses (another primary operator) after function names should have no space before them. Expressions within parentheses should be written with no space after the opening parenthesis and no space before the closing parenthesis:

```
exp(2., x)
```

The unary operators should also be written with no space between them and their operands:

```
!p   ~b   ++i   --j   -n   (long)m   *p   &x   sizeof(k)
```

The assignment operators must always have space around them, and so must the conditional operator:

```
c1 = c2              i += j              n > 0 ? n : -n
```

Commas (and semicolons) should have one space (or newline) after them:

```
strncat(t, s, n)              for (i = 0; i < n; ++i)
```

The other operators should generally be written with one space on either side of the operator:

```
x + y              a < b && b < c       m + 1
```

Occasionally, these operators may appear with no space around them, but the operators with no space around them must bind their operands tighter than the adjacent operators:

```
flag ? a : b-10              printf(fmt, a+1, b+1, c+1)
```

To summarize this standard, we will classify the operators into high precedence (primary and unary), low precedence (conditional, assignment, and comma), and medium precedence (all the others: arithmetic, bitwise, relational, logical). Using these categories, the high precedence operators never have space around them, the low precedence operators always have space around them, and the medium precedence operators usually have space around them.

Keywords (if, while, for, switch, return) should be followed by one space.

JUSTIFICATION
Readability of the code is enhanced by a uniform layout of the operators.

Spaces are related to precedence by the following observation:

> Visually, spaces connote *looser binding* than the absence of spaces. Consider the difference in meaning between "light housekeeper" and "lighthouse keeper". The same principle labels this code as misleading:

```
n = a+b * c;     /* bad - misleading spacing */
```

Automated processing of program text by editor programs and other text-searchers is possible only if spaces are rigorously formatted. Space after keywords allows easy visual distinction of control structures from function calls. Furthermore, in the syntax of C, keywords bind looser than all the operators.

[LOCAL NOTES]

NAME

2.2_evalorder - allowable dependencies on evaluation order

STANDARD

Programs should not depend upon the order of evaluation of expressions, except as guaranteed by C for the following operators:

```
1.  a, b        comma operator (not the comma between args)
2.  a && b      logical and
3.  a || b      logical or
4.  a ? b : c   conditional
```

All of these guarantee that expression a will be computed before expression b (or c). In case 4, exactly one of the two expressions b and c will be evaluated.

Furthermore, when a function-call takes place, all the arguments are fully evaluated before control transfers to the function. Thus, in

```
5.  a(b)        function-call
```

the operand b will be evaluated before the function a is called.

To this list of five guarantees, C adds one more sequence guarantee:

```
6.  each full expression
```

C guarantees that each *full expression* (the enclosing expression that is not a subexpression) will be evaluated completely before going further.

The five operators above, plus the "full expression", are the "sequence points" of C, the guarantees of sequential execution.

Commas, when used to separate arguments in a function invocation, are *not operators,* and no evaluation order should be assumed. Only the *operator* comma will guarantee order of evaluation, as in this example:

```
tmp = x[i], x[i] = x[j], x[j] = tmp;
```

Code which depends on the order of evaluation may perform differently with different compilers or different machines, may perform differently when the code generator for a given compiler is changed at some future time, and may even perform differently with the same compiler if changes to the program affect the allocation of registers.

EXAMPLE

```
if (j < MAXBOUND && a[j] == TARGET) /* ok order-dependence */

printf("%d:%d\\n", ++i, ++i); /* bad order-dependence */
```

[LOCAL NOTES]

NAME
2.3_parens - parentheses

STANDARD
Bitwise operators (& | ^ >> <<) should be explicitly parenthesized when combined with other medium-precedence operators (arithmetic, bitwise, relational, logical):

```
if ((status & MASK) != SET)
    field = (w >> OFFSET) | FLAG;
```

The embedded assignment operator must also be explicitly parenthesized in these same contexts, because of its lower precedence:

```
while ((c = getchar()) != EOF)
    ++nc;
```

For the other operators, a competent C programmer should be expected to know the precedence rules of the language, and not to insert needless parentheses routinely.

JUSTIFICATION
The precedence of bitwise operators is intrinsically ambiguous. In certain respects, they behave like arithmetic operators, producing quasi-arithmetic results. In other respects, they are like logical operators, producing a "yes-or-no" result. The simplest course is always to use parentheses with bitwise operators.

When the bitwise operators are excluded from consideration, the precedence of the other operators is natural and intuitive. The following five mnemonic rules are common, fluent C constructs:

```
a = -b + c[d]       primary and unary are obviously strongest

a + b < c + d       arithmetic is naturally stronger than relational

a < b && c < d      relational is stronger than logical

a = b ? c : d       a conditional can be assigned to something

a = b, c = d        assignments can be strung together with commas
```

Also remember that multiplicative arithmetic operators (* / %) are stronger than additive arithmetics (+ -), and that the multiplicative logical (&&) is stronger than the additive logical (||).

All these rules, when taken together, specify the precedence of C is a mnemonic way:

PRECEDENCE LEVEL	MNEMONIC EXAMPLE
primary	
unary	a = -b + c[d]
arithmetic (multiplicative)	
arithmetic (additive)	
relational	a + b < c + d
logical (multiplicative)	a < b && c < d
logical (additive)	
conditional	a = b ? c : d
assignments	
comma	a = b, c = d

[LOCAL NOTES]

NAME
2.4_rightshift - right-shift and unsigned data

STANDARD
Always cast the left-hand operand of right-shift to an unsigned type, in portable code.

JUSTIFICATION
Sign-extension is either compiler-dependent or machine-dependent. Also, right-shift as "pseudo-divide" can give wrong results for negative numbers.

EXAMPLE

```
mask = ~0 >> n;              /* bad - can give -1 result for any n */

mask = (uint)~0 >> n;        /* good - guarantees unsigned shift */
```

[LOCAL NOTES]

[LOCAL NOTES]

NAME
2.5_sideorder - order of side effects

STANDARD
Programs must not depend upon the order in which side effects take place. In particular, the postfix increment/decrement operators may alter the memory at unpredictable times during the evaluation of the expression. All that C guarantees is that the side effect will be complete when the next "sequence point" is reached (see 2.2_evalorder).

Here is a simplistic but useful rule: a variable which is the operand of increment, decrement, or embedded assignment should not have any more appearances in the same arithmetic expression.

JUSTIFICATION
Programs that depend upon the order of side effects may not perform correctly when ported to a new machine or a new compiler.

EXAMPLE

```
a[i] = i++;       /* bad - which is done first?  [] or ++ ? */

++i + i /* bad - is i changed before second i is accessed? */

n = (i = 2) + i + 5;             /* bad - i appears twice */

s[i++] = t[j++];       /* good - does not depend upon order */
```

[LOCAL NOTES]

[LOCAL NOTES]

NAME
    2.6_conv - conversions and overflow

STANDARD
    Do not depend upon the returned value from the math functions
    for detecting errors. Set the global errno to zero before the compu-
    tation, and test it afterwards. (The returned values can vary
    between implementations.) (RDS 2.1)

    Or, if possible, prevent math errors by carefully bounds-checking
    before calling functions.

    When two unsigned int's are subtracted, convert the result using
    either (uint) or UI_TO_I. (The macro UI_TO_I is simply an (int) cast,
    except in certain ones-complement environments.) (RDS 2.7)

    Use IMOD (or some similar mechanism) to ensure that a non-negative
    modulo result is produced. (RDS 2.7)

```
/* robust, slow, "unprotected" macro for IMOD: */
#define IMOD(i, j) ((i)%(j)<0 ? (i)%(j)+(j) : (i)%(j))

/* if "remainder" (%) is always non-negative, use this: */
#define IMOD(i, j) ((i) % (j))
```

    In (signed) integer arithmetic, assume that overflow is invalid, may
    be detected (hence should never be programmed), and cannot be
    trapped or ignored. (RDS 2.8)

ALTERNATIVES

    In (signed) integer arithmetic, the default assumption of most exist-
    ing C environments is that integer overflow is silently ignored. A
    project which does not foresee integer overflow trapping in its
    future environment may wish to allow silent overflows in project
    code, provided that integer expression limits are enforced with
    explicit tests. (See 5.5_defensive.)

    A project which does not foresee a future ones-complement
    environment can simply use (uint) and (int) casts upon unsigned
    subtraction.

[LOCAL NOTES]

[LOCAL NOTES]

NAME
2.7_ctype - character tests

STANDARD
Use the `<ctype.h>` facilities for character tests and upper-lower conversions. (RDS 2.3)

JUSTIFICATION
These facilities are portable across different character code sets, are usually very efficient, and provide international flexibility.

EXAMPLE

```
if ('a' <= c && c <= 'z')
        /* bad - assumes that letters are contiguous */

if (islower(c))
        /* good - portable to different character sets, */
        /* even non-English sets with extra letters */
```

[LOCAL NOTES]

[LOCAL NOTES]

NAME
   3.1_lexctl - lexical rules for control structure

STANDARD
   Each source file that conforms to these standards is formatted con-
   sistently according to one of the following styles of bracing:

```
#1: indented braces     #2: exdented braces     #3: Kernighan & Ritchie

if (a == b)             if (a == b)             if (a == b) {
    {                   {                           err("b");
    err("b");               err("b");               ++nerrs;
    ++nerrs;                ++nerrs;            }
    }                   }
```

However, an aggregate initializer which fits entirely on one line will
usually have its opening and closing braces also on that line:

```
short a[] = {1, 1, 2, 3, 5};
```

A similar exception is allowed for an aggregate declaration which
conveniently fits on one line:

```
struct complex {double real; double imag;};
```

All three bracing styles follow the same rule for the tabbing of
subordinate lines: Each line which is part of the body of a C control
structure (if, while, do-while, for, switch) is indented one tab stop
from the margin of its controlling line. The same rule applies to
function definitions, structure-or-union definitions, and aggregate
initializers. (Examples in Plum Hall textbooks follow bracing style
#1.)

Tabs should be reflected by a uniform amount of white space,
preferably four spaces. Four is better than eight because the source
listings do not tend to run off the right edge so quickly.

For code which contains no braces, the tabbing rules produce the
same result:

```
if (a == 1)
    x = y;

if (a == b)
    ++nerrs;
else
    subfn(b);
```

```
if (!legal(code))
    remark("bad code: ", code);
else if (lookup(code))
    remark("multiple definition: ", code);
else
    install(code, val);

while ((c = getchar()) != EOF)
    putchar(c);

for (;;)
    timetest(n);
```

Examples involving braces:

```
#1: indented braces    #2: exdented braces    #3: Kernighan & Ritchie

switch (c)             switch (c)
    {                  {                       switch (c) {
case '\n':             case '\n':              case '\n':
case '\r':             case '\r':              case '\r':
    echo('\n');            echo('\n');             echo('\n');
    break;                 break;                  break;
case '\t':             case '\t':              case '\t':
    tabcnt();              tabcnt();               tabcnt();
    break;                 break;                  break;
default:               default:                default:
    echo(c);               echo(c);                echo(c);
    }                  }                       }

while (p != NULL)      while (p != NULL)
    {                  {                       while (p != NULL) {
p = nxt(p);                p = nxt(p);             p = nxt(p);
++syms;                    ++syms;                 ++syms;
    }                  }                       }

do                     do
    {                  {                       do {
c = getans();              c = getans();           c = getans();
    } while (!ok(c));  } while (!ok(c));       } while (!ok(c));

struct item            struct item
    {                  {                       struct item {
char *name;                char *name;             char *name;
char *value;               char *value;            char *value;
    };                 };                      };
```

[LOCAL NOTES]

55

Nested control structures are formatted by the simple rule that the entire nested structure is indented to the margin of the surrounding body. For example:

```
while ((c = getchar()) != EOF)        /* #1: indented braces */
    {
    if (isspace(c))
        putchar('\n');
    else
        putchar(c);
    }

while ((c = getchar()) != EOF)        /* #2: exdented braces */
    {
    if (isspace(c))
        putchar('\n');
    else
        putchar(c);
    }

while ((c = getchar()) != EOF) {      /* #3: Kernighan & Ritchie */
    if (isspace(c))
        putchar('\n');
    else
        putchar(c);
    }
```

Lines within a C source file should fit a listing (or screen) width of 80 characters. Any expression that is too long to fit this size should be broken into multiple lines. The proper place to break a line is at an operator of lower precedence than those that surround it.

A null statement appearing as the body of a control structure deserves a line of its own:

```
while (*s++ != '\0')
    ;
```

In the test expression of while, for, do-while, or if, the comparison should be written explicitly, rather than relying upon the default comparison to zero:

```
while (fgets(buf, BUFSIZ, stdin) != NULL)
    process(buf);

if (system(cmd) != 0)
    fprintf(stderr, "cmd failed\n");
```

However, the comparison of bool's to zero or non-zero is most legibly written without explicit comparison:

```
if (isspace(c))
    putchar('\n');
```

And comparison of characters to null characters, and pointers to null pointers, can be written as an implicit comparison, if a long or repetitive control line can be simplified thereby:

```
for (p = head; p && p->next && p->next->next; p = p->next)
    install(p);
```

Mistaking the single equal-sign assignment operator for the double equal-sign comparison operator is one of the most common C bugs. An embedded assignment in a test expression should always be tested explicitly:

```
while (*s++ = *t++)            /* BAD - resembles equality */
    ;

while ((*s++ = *t++) != '\0')   /* GOOD - avoids confusion */
    ;
```

JUSTIFICATION

There is, unfortunately, more emotional argument among C fans about the placement of braces than about any other single style issue. The issue ultimately is only a matter of personal opinion, but the adherants of each preference have reasons which are compelling to them. The basic position of these guidelines is that consistency within the individual project is quite an adequate level of standardization.

Most of the other rules of this section are chosen to minimize common mistakes in coding. Some aspects of consistent layout are intended to facilitate the use of automated text-handling tools.

ALTERNATIVES

Some organizations have frequent maintenance to many small projects, and prefer one organization-wide layout standard, rather than project-by-project choices.

[LOCAL NOTES]

NAME
3.2_while - while and the N+1/4 - time loop

STANDARD
Side effects are explicitly allowed in the test of while or for. The underlying flow chart shows a box that is executed N+1 times whenever the lower box is executed N times, so the loop is known as an "N+1/2 - time" loop. In C, the upper box is only an expression, whereas the lower box is an entire statement, so the loop can be called an "N+1/4 - time" loop.

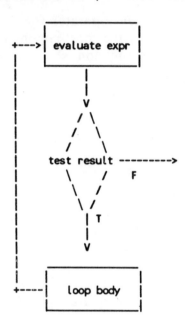

JUSTIFICATION
Such side effects are one of the *strengths* of C; they smoothly handle a large proportion of common loops. They almost eliminate the awkward "duplicated read" loops, yet they require no complicated "lookahead" mechanism.

[LOCAL NOTES]

[LOCAL NOTES]

NAME
3.3_loopinvar - designing with loop invariants

GUIDELINE
The "invariant condition" of a loop is a "typical picture" of the loop variables, a relationship which

o   is always true at each iteration of the loop, and still true at loop termination; and

o   guarantees that the goal of the loop is attained when the loop terminates.

Consider this familiar loop:

```
while ((c = getchar()) != EOF)
    putchar(c);
```

The invariant condition is "A series of n characters have been read and already printed out in sequence, and one more character c has been read but not yet printed." This condition is true at the start of the loop; and if it is true for n iterations, after we go around the loop once more, it becomes true for $n+1$. The condition guarantees that the goal of the loop is attained at termination, because when c is EOF, all the characters from beginning to end of file have been read and printed.

Graphically, this invariant condition, or "typical picture" looks like this:

```
Already read:        _ _ ... _ _
                              c

Already printed:     _ _ ... _
```

There may be portions of the loop body during which this "typical picture" is not true (as the variables are altered). For example, in the getchar loop above, the picture is not strictly true just after c is printed and just before getchar delivers the new c. These portions are the "domain of exceptions".

The program will be *more readable* if the *domain of exceptions is minimized*.

[LOCAL NOTES]

[LOCAL NOTES]

JUSTIFICATION

Altering the relationship between variables during a loop increases the complexity of the reader's task. The more complex the loop, the greater the need for this uniformity.

"Minimizing the domain of exceptions" gives an explicit justification for the experienced programmer's intuition that certain forms of for loops are preferable; they confine the domain of exceptions to the for line.

EXAMPLE

```
for (p = head; p != NULL; p = p->next)
    {
    /* invariant - p points to current item for processing */
    ... process p
    }

for (pp = &head; *pp && (*pp)->next; pp = &(*pp)->next)
    {
    /* invariant -
     *  *pp is pointer to current item, and
     *  (*pp)->next is pointer to the item after it;
     *  insert/delete can be done by altering *pp;
     *  both are non-NULL
     */
    ... process *pp and (*pp)->next
    }
```

[LOCAL NOTES]

[LOCAL NOTES]

NAME
3.4_elseif - multiple-choice constructs

STANDARD
The else-if should be used for multiple-choice constructs whenever the conditions are not mutually exclusive, whenever their order of evaluation is important, or whenever they test different variables. Otherwise, use the switch.

Do not make up artificial variables just to make use of a switch.

In either case, each alternative action is tabbed to the same indent.

In a switch, each group of statements should end with a break before the next case label. In unusual cases, it is allowable for one group of statements to "flow-through" into the next label, but a standard comment such as

```
/* flow-through */
```

must appear in place of the break.

ALTERNATIVES
In addition to the rules above, each switch can be required to specify an explicit (possibly empty) default case. Some projects have found this useful for bug-prevention.

JUSTIFICATION
Although the else-if could always be used instead of switch, the distinction is helpful for readability. The efficiency of switch is sometimes significant. The indentation shows the logical nature of the multiple-choice.

EXAMPLE

```
if (!legal(code))
    remark("bad code: ", code);
else if (lookup(code))
    remark("multiple definition: ", code);
else
    install(code, val);
```

```
switch (sc)
    {
case EXTERN:
    remark("redefined", "");
    break;
case LOCAL:
    osc = LOCAL;
    /* flow-through */
case STATIC:
    printf("...");
    break;
case INTERN:
    printf("...");
    sc = STATIC;
    break;
default:
    remark("unknown sc", "");
    }
```

[LOCAL NOTES]

NAME
3.5_control - restrictions on control structures

STANDARD
The goto statement (and hence labels as well) should not be used.

The while loop should be used instead of the do-while loop, except where the logic of the problem explicitly requires doing the body at least once regardless of the loop condition.

If a single if-else can replace a continue, an if-else should be used.

JUSTIFICATION
The goto statement is prohibited for the empirical reason that its use is highly correlated with errors and hard-to-read code, and for the abstract reason that algorithms should be expressed in structures that facilitate checking the program against the structure of the underlying process. (See 3.6_structure for detailed explanation; see 0.1_standards regarding occasional exceptions.)

The do-while is discouraged because loops should be coded in such a form as to "do nothing gracefully"; i.e. they should test their looping condition before executing the body.

[LOCAL NOTES]

[LOCAL NOTES]

NAME
3.6_structure - program structure and problem structure

GUIDELINE
The structure of the data being processed (expressed in augmented BNF — "Backus Normal Form"— or equivalent notation) should match the structure of the program.

Sequence:

If the data structure is

> $a \quad b \quad c$

(which means "items a, b, and c in that order") the program structure will be a sequence, such as

```
process a; process b; process c;
```

Choice:

If the data structure is

> $a \mid b$

(which means "choice between a or b") the program structure will be a conditional, such as

```
if (data is a)
    process a;
else
    process b;
```

Repetition:

If the problem structure is

> a^*

(which means "repetition of the item a") the program structure will be a loop, such as

```
while (more a)
    process a;
```

or

```
for (first a; more a; next a)
    process a;
```

[LOCAL NOTES]

[LOCAL NOTES]

JUSTIFICATION
The usefulness of syntax-oriented design has been well-established in practice. Writing down the data syntax helps get the problem clear. The data syntax gives a reliable outline for the first draft of the program. And the process of checking the resulting program against the data syntax aids in the review.

Useful readings are found in Jackson (1975), Warnier (1974), and Wirth (1973).

EXAMPLE
Data structure is

$$\{\, a \mid b \mid c\, \}^{*}$$

(which means "a repetition of a choice among a, b, and c")

Program structure is

```
while (get an item)
    {
    if (its type is A)
        process type-A code;
    else if (its type is B)
        process type-B code;
    else if (its type is C)
        process type-C code;
    else
        error("invalid code: ", code);
    }
```

[LOCAL NOTES]

[LOCAL NOTES]

NAME
4.1_lexfns - lexical rules for functions

STANDARD

External declarations and function definitions begin at the left margin (with optional storage class and mandatory type). An explanatory comment is required before each function, and is also at the left margin.

All functions are declared in "new-style" Standard C prototype format, with parameter names and types appearing within the parentheses of the definition. A typical one-function file looks like this:

Style #1, indented braces:

```
#include "local.h"
TYPEX varx = NNN;    /* comment describing varx */

/* comment describing func
 */
TYPE func(
    TYPE1 a1,    /* comment describing a1 */
    TYPE2 a2)    /* comment describing a2 */
    {
    <local declarations>

    <statements>
    }
```

Style #2, exdented braces, and style #3, Kernighan & Ritchie:

```
#include "local.h"
TYPEX varx = NNN;    /* comment describing varx */

/* comment describing func
 */
TYPE func(
TYPE1 a1,    /* comment describing a1 */
TYPE2 a2)    /* comment describing a2 */
{
    <local declarations>

    <statements>
}
```

The blank line between local declarations and statements is omitted if no local declarations are present.

In portable programs, the `main` function should be defined with no parameters, or with two parameters:

```
int main()
    {
    /* ... */
    }

int main(argc, argv)
    int argc;
    char *argv[];
    {
    /* ... */
    }
```

UNIX systems provide a third parameter (conventionally named `envp`) and a global pointer (named `environ`). Values in the "environment" can be changed using the `putenv` function. Neither `envp` nor `environ` nor `putenv` are portable to Standard C or other non-UNIX C.

JUSTIFICATION

This layout is chosen for consistency with the layout of control structures described in 3.1_lexctl. The essential feature here, as there, is the uniform indentation of the body and the alignment of the braces above and below the body.

The main advantages of preserving the "old C" layout of one parameter per source line are to preserve line numbering after translation into "new style", and to provide space for comments documenting each function parameter.

ALTERNATIVES

If function parameters are documented somewhere other than in the function definition itself, the function definition can be abbreviated in the new prototype style:

```
TYPE func(TYPE1 a1, TYPE2 a2)
    {
    /* etc. ... */
    }
```

Some projects prefer function-names at the left margin, with the return-type on the previous line. Some prefer mandatory `void` in no-parameter function definitions; some always leave it out. (It is important for prototype *declarations*, but makes little difference on definitions.)

[LOCAL NOTES]

73

NAME
    4.2_headers - project-wide standard headers

STANDARD
    All programs within a project should use a locally-written header designed for use by that project; this file is generically referred to as local.h in this book. This file should #include, typedef and #define everything of general usefulness for the project.

    Using a local standard header can allow portable code to be compiled for different environments. The environment-dependent definitions in the header may have to change, but the source code of the application will not have to change.

    There should be one designated header directory (or a small list of directories) for each project. Each header can then be accessed in the project header directory.

    All definitions of compile-time values and of structure formats should be put into headers if they are shared by more than one file.

    Reliable modification of defined constants requires an environmental capability: there must be a means for ensuring that all files comprising a program have been compiled using the same set of headers. (The UNIX make command is one such capability.) (RDS 1.1)

[LOCAL NOTES]

[LOCAL NOTES]

Headers unique to a project are allowed, and are included via

```
#include "file.h"
```

All other headers will be included via the "angle-brackets" notation:

```
#include <file.h>
```

Name formats specific to one operating system (such as `[1,1]file.h` or `<subdir/file.h>`) prevent portability to other systems, and are disallowed in portable code. For maximal portability, use no more than six lower-case letters followed by ".h".

JUSTIFICATION

The choice of header environments requires some skill and experience, and is often best made by team leaders or senior programmers. The inclusion of a single `local.h` file is then easier for standardization than the specification of a list of `#include`'s and `#define`'s. Rigorous use of `#ifndef...#endif` sandwiches around headers (see 4.6_nest) will eliminate the most common objection to project-wide headers, namely that they made multiply-included files more likely.

The names defined in project-wide headers (either directly or via nested `#include`) are, in effect, reserved words for that project; even if a programmer makes no use of some group of names, later modifications to the program might introduce them. Name conflicts should be discovered early if possible.

During development, it often becomes necessary to rearrange the directory structure. Avoiding absolute file names minimizes the tedious re-editing of the `#include`'s.

Different versions of a project can have different `#include` environments without introducing problems of retroactively modifying existing code.

Since function prototypes declare function parameters, it is important that functions are declared before being called. Putting each function declaration into an associated header (as is done in the Standard Library) is the most reliable way.

[LOCAL NOTES]

[LOCAL NOTES]

EXAMPLE

Assume that version 1.1 of project *a* has collected its local headers into directory /xx/projecta.1.1, which contains local.h and specific.h. In the file pgm.c we will find these #include statements:

```
#include "local.h"
#include "specific.h"
```

It may be useful to create a project-wide compile command which specifies this directory as the location of header files; assuming that this command is named proja.cc, we can compile pgm.c like this:

```
proja.cc pgm.c
```

ALTERNATIVES

Programs for general publication (in articles or newsletters) should use a minimal set of generally-available headers. Only these headers provided by Standard C should be assumed in general-publication programs.

[LOCAL NOTES]

[LOCAL NOTES]

NAME
   4.3_files - size of source files

STANDARD
   Source files should be no larger than 500 lines.

JUSTIFICATION
   Experience has shown that larger files are cumbersome to edit
   correctly and to maintain.

ALTERNATIVES
   On large mainframe systems, a more commonly-used limit is 1000
   lines.

[LOCAL NOTES]

[LOCAL NOTES]

NAME
   4.4_includes - put includes at head of file

STANDARD
   Each source file should start with its list of #include's grouped at the
   head of the file, before any declarations or function definitions.
   After the #include's, next come any #define's needed for the file.

   However, it may sometimes be necessary for a #define to precede the
   #include's (to control conditional inclusion). Putting the #define first
   will emphasize that it affects the #include'd files.

JUSTIFICATION
   Headers form the context for the code in the file. Grouping them
   together allows quick verification of the list, and facilitates any
   necessary dependency-checking.

EXAMPLE

```
#include "local.h"
#include "specific.h"

#define GOODCODE 1
#define BADCODE 0
/* now comes the rest of the program */
```

[LOCAL NOTES]

[LOCAL NOTES]

NAME
4.5_stdflags - standard compile-time flags

STANDARD
Standard compile-time flags should be chosen project-wide for environmental issues such as target machine, target operating system, and debug options. Such flags should not be hard-coded into the program (unless required by its environment-specific function), because they can be turned on by command line option.

JUSTIFICATION
Judiciously chosen conditional definitions allow efficient targeting of such issues as word size, byte size, and specific forms for system interfaces such as file control blocks, etc. Selective trace and assertion functions can be included with ease if a flag such as NDEBUG is available to turn off code production when not wanted.

[LOCAL NOTES]

[LOCAL NOTES]

NAME
    4.6_nest - nested headers

STANDARD
    To avoid multiple inclusions of the contents of a header, each
    header should begin with a #ifndef that tests whether some #define'd
    symbol has already been defined, and should end with #endif. (RDS
    1.6)

    Each header should #include any other headers whose definitions are
    assumed. If possible, the header should test, with #ifndef, whether
    the #include is necessary.

JUSTIFICATION
    The contents of each header should be included only once during
    each compilation. If the #include's are nested unconditionally, this
    property becomes hard to control.

    Making the #include itself to be conditional can improve the speed
    of compilations.

EXAMPLE

```
local.h:

    #ifndef LOCAL_H
    #define LOCAL_H

    #ifndef BUFSIZ
    #include <stdio.h>
    #endif

    ... other definitions

    #endif
```

[LOCAL NOTES]

[LOCAL NOTES]

NAME
    4.7_noinit - no initializations in headers

STANDARD
    Headers should not contain initialization of anything.

JUSTIFICATION
    Putting the initialization in a header doesn't make clear which func-
    tion "owns" the data; i.e., it doesn't localize the "defining
    instance".

    Multiple source files each including a file containing initializations
    will, in general, produce "multiply defined" diagnostics.

    In general, programmers should be assured that #include'ing various
    headers will not increase their object-code size.

EXAMPLE
        defs.h:

```
#ifndef DEFS_H
#define DEFS_H
typedef short TOKEN;
typedef struct tokitem TOKITEM;
struct tokitem
    {
    char *name;
    TOKEN val;
    };
#endif
```

    Method 1 - If there is one file that contains functions which will
    always be needed if the data is referenced, put the definition into
    that file:

        tablemgr.c:

```
TOKITEM tokt =
    {
    "pin", 1,
    "wire", 2,
    /* ... */
    };
    /* ... */
```

    followed by functions which process the data.

Method 2 - If no one file "owns" the data, put the definition in a file of its own, which gives a "data-only" object-file which will be linked when needed by any of several functions:

```
tokt.c:

TOKITEM tokt =
    {
    /* ... */
    };
```

[LOCAL NOTES]

NAME

4.8_coupling - methods of coupling modules together

STANDARD

Data that is to be shared by two functions should be local (external static) unless global linkage is specifically necessary.

The preferred method for cross-function communication is the passing of arguments. However, "pass-through" parameters, whose only function is to pass data downward to called functions, create a problem for both readability and maintainability. If two or more levels of pass-through are required, use either external data or "package" modules (LPC 6.). Also, certain data of an "environmental" or "context" nature is more conveniently handled as a "default" value. For example, the standard I/O functions (getchar, putchar, printf, etc.) make use of globally-known values for stdin and stdout. The mechanism to override the default is also available (getc, putc, fprintf, etc.) for cases in which the default is not appropriate.

JUSTIFICATION

Integration problems are made more probable by each global linkage. See Yourdon & Constantine (1978) for lengthier (!) justification.

[LOCAL NOTES]

[LOCAL NOTES]

NAME
4.9_cohesion - cohesion and meaningful functions

STANDARD
A function should evidence "functional cohesiveness" (Yourdon & Constantine, 1978), which can be adequately summarized by the following test:

> Can the purpose of the function be accurately summarized by a sentence in the form
>
> "specific verb + specific object(s)"?

This sentence should appear in a comment just before the function.

JUSTIFICATION
The logic of the calling module can be verified only if the action of each called function can be grasped without having to resort to line-by-line reading.

[LOCAL NOTES]

[LOCAL NOTES]

NAME
4.10_libfns - file structure for library functions

STANDARD

General-purpose functions (i.e., functions callable by more than one `main`) should be placed in separate source files.

General-purpose functions must be documented and maintained as library functions, including a manual-page specification.

Each such file should contain at its end a `main` function which will try out the called function. This test driver should be surrounded by a `#ifdef` and `#endif` keyed to a compilation flag (e.g., `TRYMAIN`) chosen project-wide.

In portable programs, the names of the Standard Library functions should be treated as reserved words. In other words, do not make a new function named `fopen`, even if its behavior is supposed to mimic the Standard `fopen` function.

JUSTIFICATION

Object files are created on a per-source-file basis. Calling programs should not inadvertently link multiple functions when they need only one function.

Standardizing the format of tryout functions and putting them into the source reduces the number of files to be maintained and places examples of use in a place where they are most likely to be seen.

EXAMPLE

This example illustrates possible source code for the Standard Library function strcmp, which is obliged in Standard C to use unsigned comparisons. (For the rationale behind the choice of test cases, see 7.1_reviews.)

```
/* strcmp - compare (unsigned) strings */
int strcmp(
    register const char s[],   /* : string */
    register const char t[])   /* : string */
    {
    typedef unsigned char uchar;

    while (*s != '\0' && *s == *t)
        {
        ++s;
        ++t;
        }
    if (*(uchar *)s < *(uchar *)t))
        return -1;
    else if (*(uchar *)s == *(uchar *)t)
        return 0;
    else
        return 1;
    }
#ifdef TRYMAIN
#include <limits.h>
#include <assert.h>
#undef NDEBUG   /* turn on assert's */
char s_max[2] = {UCHAR_MAX, '\0'};  /* string with largest uchar */
int main()
    {
    assert(strcmp("", s_max) < 0);   /* case 1 */
    assert(strcmp("a", "a") == 0);   /* case 2 */
    assert(strcmp(s_max, "") > 0);   /* case 3 */
    exit(0);
    }
#endif
```

[LOCAL NOTES]

95

NAME
   4.11_portlib - use of portable library

STANDARD

A portable program interacts with its environment through the library interfaces that are chosen by the project. Other than these library capabilities, a portable program should not assume anything else about its environment.

See Section 6 for details of the Standard Library.

Do not assume system-specific I/O formats.

Do not assume availability of system commands.

Do not assume system-specific command-invocations (e.g. UNIX exec).

The files stdin, stdout, and stderr are provided by the Standard Library, and should be used whenever appropriate:

stdin   standard input (should be meaningful for file or terminal)

stdout   standard output (either file or terminal)

stderr   standard error output (all error messages should be sent to stderr).

The "low-level" I/O functions (open, close, read, write, lseek) should not be called directly in strictly portable programs. These functions are not part of Standard C, and in those systems that do support them, there are numerous small variations in functionality. For the limited task of performing binary I/O on direct-access ("disk") files, a local header (named, e.g. bin_io.h) can provide portable definitions for the names bin_open, bin_close, bin_read, bin_write, and bin_lseek. As with several of the other headers, the contents of bin_io.h may require tailoring to each environment, but the programs that use its functions will themselves be portable. (RDS 8.5) See 4.19_headers in these guidelines for an example of bin_io.h.)

The Standard Library provides some portable support for binary I/O; see the fopen function in 6.14_stdio.

JUSTIFICATION

Occasional use "for convenience" of handy system-specific functions may create serious portability problems later. The new system may not have the same formats or commands as the old system.

[LOCAL NOTES]

NAME
   4.12_environ - non-portable environment features

STANDARD
   In portable application code, segregate environment-specific code
   into separate functions or separate headers. Keep such functions as
   small and limited as possible. All other factors being equal, choose
   the method with the later binding time.

JUSTIFICATION
   This minimizes the work in porting to a new environment.

EXAMPLE

```
prefix = "/proj/dictionary/";
        /* bad - wires-in specific system */

#include "environ.h"
prefix = DICTIONARY_NAME;
        /* good - now only the header needs changing */

getnam(prefix);
        /* good - dependency is in small function */

prefix = getenv("DICTIONARY_NAME");
        /* good - postpones binding time to run-time */

config_file_name = getenv("CONFIG_FILE");
/* open configuration file, and read prefix from config_file ... */
fgets(prefix, sizeof(prefix), config_fp);
        /* good - uses run-time binding, with only one */
        /* name to clutter the environment-name space  */
```

[LOCAL NOTES]

Copyright © Plum Hall Inc 1989

[LOCAL NOTES]

NAME
    4.13_fnsize - suggested size of functions

GUIDELINE
    Programs should be designed so that most of the functions will be smaller than 50 lines of source listing.

    This guideline does not require artificial splitting of cohesive code into small pieces.

    On the other hand, code which consists of nothing but large-function files usually reveals insufficient attention to design prior to launching into code.

JUSTIFICATION
    Algorithms are easier to create and to understand if they are built of pieces small enough to be grasped as one concept.

    The 50-line guideline is derived from empirical observation of well-crafted C code.

[LOCAL NOTES]

[LOCAL NOTES]

NAME
    4.14_macros - writing macros

STANDARD
    A "protected" macro is fully parenthesized and evaulates each
    argument exactly once, so it gives a result that is equivalent to a
    function call. These "protected" macros should be documented like
    functions, and given names in lower case.

    "Unprotected" macros should be given names all in upper case.
    Examples from `local.h`:

```
MAX(x, y)        MIN(x, y)        ABS(x)
```

    When writing macros, be sure to put parentheses around the entire
    replacement text, to guard against operator precedence surprises.
    Also, each appearance of a parameter should have either
    parenthesis or comma on either side.

```
#define STREQ(s, t) (strcmp(s, t) == 0)      /* good */

#define SQUARE(x)   ((x) * (x))               /* good */
#define SQUARE(x)   x * x                     /* bad */

f = z / SQUARE(y + 1);
```

    When documenting "unprotected" macros with a manual page, be
    sure to indicate a "NOTES" or "CAVEAT" entry, warning that the
    name is an "unprotected" macro and that no side effects should
    appear on its arguments.

JUSTIFICATION
    The problems with side effects cause macros to behave differently
    from functions. The user must be protected when possible, and
    otherwise warned.

[LOCAL NOTES]

[LOCAL NOTES]

NAME
4.15_structs - defined-types for structures

STANDARD
Frequently-referenced structures and unions may be given defined-type names in upper-case letters. If the members are "hidden" from the user (simulating an "abstract data type"), then the upper-case name *must* be created.

The definition of such names (and the associated struct-or-union tags) should be in an appropriate header, unless the name is intrinsically local to only one source file.

In either event, the declaration of structure variables should be separate from the definition of the tag.

EXAMPLE

```
typedef struct task TASK;
struct task
    {
    TASK *next;
    char *desc;
    long plan, start, finish;
    };

TASK ti, tj, tk;
```

JUSTIFICATION
Combining structure tag definition with variable declaration increases the probability that the components of a structure could later be changed without finding all occurrences of that structure, so the practice is not recommended.

The naming convention is consistent with the upper-case names of locally-defined types, and historically consistent with the FILE type from <stdio.h>. As a minor extra advantage, it allows later changing of type from structure to union or scalar (or vice-versa) without extensive source code modification.

The advantage of typedef for creating the defined-type name is that syntax errors can sometimes produce more intelligible diagnostics.

[LOCAL NOTES]

[LOCAL NOTES]

NAME

4.16_stdarg - functions of a variable number of arguments

STANDARD

Functions should, in general, have a fixed number of arguments, each having a specified type.

In some exceptional situations, however, it is useful to create a function which has a variable number of arguments, or an argument of a varying type, or both. The macros in <stdarg.h> should be used for all functions which accept a varying number of arguments. (See 6.13_stdarg for details.)

JUSTIFICATION

This is the only portable way to handle varying numbers of arguments. It is also more readable than most system-specific methods.

[LOCAL NOTES]

[LOCAL NOTES]

NAME
    4.17_ptrparms - pointer parameters

STANDARD
    The default requirement for pointer parameters is that they must
    point to storage that is entirely defined (i.e., not uninitialized gar-
    bage). Whenever a pointer parameter can accept something else,
    this should be explicitly stated on that parameter's declaration com-
    ment. (RDS 4.2)

    The requirements on pointer parameters depend upon their usage:
    "out-only" pointers are used to modify memory, and not to inspect;
    "in-only" pointers are used to inspect but not modify; "in-out"
    pointers are used both to inspect and to modify. Regarding param-
    eters which are pointers to structures, an "out-only" pointer param-
    eter is assumed to be non-NULL pointing to the storage for a structure
    of the specified type. "In-only" and "in-out" pointer parameters
    are assumed to point to a well-defined structure of the specified
    type. Any exceptions should be noted in a comment on the param-
    eter declaration. (RDS 6.7)

    Standard C provides a new keyword — const — for objects which
    should not be modified. For example, the declaration

        const char *pc;

    declares that pc points to a const char. A Standard C compiler would
    diagnose any attempt to modify *p (the object that p points to).
    Therefore, both in prototypes and also in function definitions, an
    "in-only" pointer should be declared using const.

    Follow a consistent notation for pointer parameters. Either (1)
    declare all of them as *p (with the asterisk), or (2) use p[] for
    parameters designating arrays that do not overlap each other, and
    use *p for everything else. (RDS 3.4)

JUSTIFICATION
    The Plum Hall books follow the second convention for pointer
    declarations, because it conveys important semantic information,
    because some new compilers reward this style with better optimiza-
    tion, and because it generalizes more gracefully to multi-
    dimensional arrays, such as p[][10].

[LOCAL NOTES]

[LOCAL NOTES]

NAME
    4.18_reliable - reliability guidelines for functions

GUIDELINE
    The header `rdslib.h` declares some functions which illustrate useful reliability guidelines. (RDS 1.3) These are the functions:

`bool itoa(int n, char str[], int ndigits);`

    Convert the integer `n` into text-character representation in string `str`. The maximum number of digit-spaces available in `str` is given by `ndigits`. If `n` is too large to fit, represent it with a string of `ndigits` repetitions of '9', and return `NO`. Otherwise, return `YES`.

`int fgetsnn(char str[], int size, FILE *fp);`

    Read a line of at most `size-1` characters using file pointer `fp` into string `str`. If a newline is encountered within `size-1` characters, it terminates the read, but is not stored in the string. If end-of-file is encountered, return `EOF`. Otherwise, return the number of characters stored.

`int getsnn(char str[], int size);`

    Behaves like `fgetsnn(str, size, stdin)`.

`int getreply(const char prompt[], char reply[], int size);`

    Print the `prompt` string to stdout. Then read `reply` using `getsnn(reply, size)`. If `getsnn` did not encounter a newline, consume input characters until a newline. Return the length of the `reply` string, or `EOF`.

`bool getpstr(const char p[], char s[], size_t n);`

    If the next non-whitespace characters from stdin match equal to the string `p`, then read one subsequent "word" of input into the string `s` (chopped to maximum size `n`). Return `YES` if string `p` was matched, `NO` otherwise.

`bool getplin(const char p[], char s[], size_t n);`

    The behavior is the same as `getpstr`, except that the entire remainder of the input line is copied to string `s`.

`void reverse(char s[]);`

    Reverse the characters of `s` end-for-end in place.

`bool strfit(char s1[], const char s2[], size_t n);`

    Copy string `s2` into string `s1`, truncating if necessary to maximum size `n`. Return `YES` if the entire string fits into `s1`, `NO` otherwise. The resulting contents of `s1` are guaranteed to be null-terminated.

These are the guidelines exemplified by these functions:

Provide explicit bounds-checking in the function interface: All the functions that store strings provide a specification of maximum size, unlike the standard library function strcpy.

Keep data in a consistent state: The strfit function ensures that the result remains null-terminated, unlike the standard function strncpy.

Make explicit provision for the possibility of overflow, as exemplified by itoa.

Keep a file in a consistent state: The getreply function makes sure to consume all the line up to a newline, unlike scanf.

Make the calling function's validation tests easy: getpstr, getplin, and strfit all return a simple bool result.

Provide access to useful subfunctions that are used in each package: The reverse function is used by itoa, so it is documented as part of the package.

[LOCAL NOTES]

NAME
4.19_headers - contents of local standard headers

GUIDELINE
This section will present the contents of the headers suggested for use in portable programs, besides those of the Standard Library.

The header portdefs.h (discussed in 1.3_stdtypes and elsewhere) encapsulates the environment-dependent defined-types and macros:

```
/* portdefs.h - definitions for portability */
/* ENVIRONMENT-DEPENDENT - ADJUST TO LOCAL SYSTEM */
#ifndef PORTDEFS_H
#define PORTDEFS_H

#ifndef BUFSIZ
#include <stdio.h>  /* to get stderr address */
#endif

#ifndef offsetof
#include <stddef.h> /* to get offsetof */
#endif

#ifndef EXIT_SUCCESS
#include <stdlib.h> /* to get EXIT_* */
#endif

/* index_t - this type is chosen by the project */
typedef int             index_t;

/* the values for STDIN, STDOUT, STDERR (for file descriptors)
 * are not part of Standard C, and may need to be changed
 */
#define STDIN          0
#define STDOUT         1
#define STDERR         2

/* UI_TO_I - convert unsigned number to signed */
#define UI_TO_I(ui) (int)(ui)   /* OK for twos-complement */

/* NAM_LEN_EXTERNAL - length of external names */
#define NAM_LEN_EXTERNAL 31 /* could be reduced, even to 6 */
```

```
/* IMOD - modulo function giving non-negative result */
#define IMOD(i, j) ((i)%(j)<0 ? (i)%(j)+(j) : (i)%(j))
/* if "remainder" (%) is always non-negative, use this: */
/* #define IMOD(i, j) ((i) % (j)) */


/* STRICTEST_ALIGNMENT - which type has strictest alignment requirement */
#define STRICTEST_ALIGNMENT double  /* adjust for each environment */


/* the remaining definitions are the same for any Standard C compiler */
typedef signed char     schar;
typedef unsigned char   uchar;
typedef unsigned short  ushort;
typedef unsigned int    uint;
typedef unsigned long   ulong;
typedef int             bool;      /* could be char : bool */
typedef short           metachar;  /* could be int : metachar */


/* BOUNDOF - boundary alignment of type t inside a struct */
#define BOUNDOF(t) \
    ((char *)&(struct {char b0; t bn;} *)stderr)->bn \
    - (char *)stderr) /* stderr  is simply a convenient address */


/* FREE -  free p, then set p to NULL */
#define FREE(p)  (free(p), p = NULL)


/* The remaining definitions are no longer needed in the
 * Standard C (Second Edition) materials from Plum Hall,
 * but are kept here to provide backward compatibility.
typedef void *data_ptr;
typedef uchar tbool;
typedef uchar tbits;
typedef ushort bits;
typedef ulong lbits;
typedef signed char tiny;
typedef unsigned char utiny;
#define OFFSET(st, m) offsetof(st, m)
#define STRUCTASST(a, b) ((a) = (b))
#define PARMS(x) x
#define LURSHIFT(m, n) ((ulong)(m) >> (n))
#define FAIL            EXIT_FAILURE
#define SUCCEED         EXIT_SUCCESS
#endif /* PORTDEFS_H */
```

Some of these definitions will need adjustment to reflect the
characteristics of each environment; they are grouped at the head
of the file. The other definitions should be suitable for any Standard C environment.

The header rdslib.h (discussed in 4.18_reliable) declares functions used in *Reliable Data Structures in C*:

```
#ifndef RDSLIB_H
#define RDSLIB_H

#ifndef PORTDEFS_H
#include "portdefs.h"    /* to get  bool  and  size_t */
#endif

bool itoa(int n, char str[], int ndigits);
int fgetsnn(char str[], int size, FILE *fp);
int getsnn(char str[], int size);
int getreply(const char p[], char reply[], int size);
bool getpstr(const char p[], char s[], size_t n);
bool getplin(const char p[], char s[], size_t n);
void reverse(char s[]);
bool strfit(char s1[], char s2[], size_t n);
#endif /* RDSLIB_H */
```

As discussed in 4.2_headers, the "local" standard header will #include a selection of Standard headers, to provide a uniform environment across different systems. The Standard headers <assert.h>, <ctype.h>, <errno.h>, <float.h>, <limits.h>, <math.h>, <stddef.h>, <stdlib.h>, <stdio.h>, <string.h>, and <time.h> are included directly from the vendor-supplied Standard C headers.

The Standard headers <locale.h>, <setjmp.h>, <signal.h>, and <stdarg.h> are not suggested for use in the "local" standard header. They can be #include'd on an as-needed basis in each application.

Contents of the generic "local" header, local.h:

```
/* local.h - local standard header file */
#ifndef LOCAL_H
#define LOCAL_H

#ifndef assert
#include <assert.h>
#endif

#ifndef isalpha
#include <ctype.h>
#endif

#ifndef EDOM
#include <errno.h>
#endif

#ifndef DBL_MAX
#include <float.h>
#endif

#ifndef INT_MAX
#include <limits.h>
#endif

#ifndef HUGE_VAL
#include <math.h>
#endif

#ifndef offsetof
#include <stddef.h>
#endif

#ifndef EXIT_SUCCESS
#include <stdlib.h>
#endif

#ifndef BUFSIZ
#include <stdio.h>
#endif

#include <string.h>

#ifndef CLOCKS_PER_SEC
#include <time.h>
#endif
```

```
#define FALSE          0           /* : bool */
#define FOREVER        for (;;)     /* endless loop */
#define NO             0           /* : bool */
#define TRUE           1           /* : bool */
#define YES            1           /* : bool */
#define getln(s, n)    ((fgets(s, n, stderr)==NULL) ? EOF : strlen(s))
#define ABS(x)         (((x) < 0) ? -(x) : (x))
#define MAX(x, y)      (((x) < (y)) ? (y) : (x))
#define MIN(x, y)      (((x) < (y)) ? (x) : (y))
#define DIM(a)         (sizeof(a) / sizeof(a[0]))
#define IN_RANGE(n, lo, hi) ((lo) <= (n) && (n) <= (hi))

#define asserts(cond, str) assert(cond) /* use Standard C assert macro */
#define SWAP(a, b, t)  ((t) = (a), (a) = (b), (b) = (t))
#define LOOPDN(r, n)   for ((r) = (n)+1; --(r) > 0; )
#define STREQ(s, t)    (strcmp(s, t) == 0)
#define STRLT(s, t)    (strcmp(s, t) < 0)
#define STRGT(s, t)    (strcmp(s, t) > 0)
#include "portdefs.h"  /* portability definitions */
#include "rdslib.h"    /* functions from Reliable Data Structures in C */
#endif  /* LOCAL_H */
```

An alternative used by some projects replaces STREQ, STRLT, and STRGT with one macro STR:

```
#define STR(s, OP, t) (strcmp(s, t) OP 0)
```

This is used, for example, like this:

```
if (STR(reply, ==, "y"))

    /* ... or ... */

while (STR(account, <=, current))
```

Contents of the "binary I/O" header, bin_io.h:

```
/* bin_io.h - header for binary file I/O functions
 * ENVIRONMENT-DEPENDENT - ADJUST TO LOCAL SYSTEM
 */
#ifndef BIN_IO_H
#define BIN_IO_H

#ifndef LOCAL_H
#include "local.h"
#endif

#ifndef O_RDONLY
#include "fcntl.h"       /* provide your own if needed */
#endif

typedef int bin_fd;      /* "binary file descriptor" */

#define BIN_NFILE 20     /* adjust to local system */

#define O_RWMODE (O_RDONLY|O_WRONLY|O_RDWR)
                         /* uses symbols from fcntl.h */

#define bin_open(s, m)     open(s, m)
#define bin_close(f)       close(f)
#define bin_lseek(f, o, w) lseek(f, o, w)
#define bin_read(f, b, n)  read(f, b, n)
#define bin_write(f, b, n) write(f, b, n)

#endif  /* BIN_IO_H */
```

The header bin_io.h needs another system-dependent header, fcntl.h:

```
/* fcntl.h - definitions for binary  open
 * Compatible with UNIX Sys V, ...
 * SYSTEM DEPENDENT - ADJUST FOR LOCAL SYSTEM
 * (Or use the one provided on local system, if available.)
 */
#ifndef FCNTL_H
#define FCNTL_H
#define O_RDONLY 0
#define O_WRONLY 1
#define O_RDWR   2
#define O_NDELAY 4       /* not used by bin_io */
#define O_APPEND 8
#define O_CREAT  0x100
#define O_TRUNC  0x200
#define O_EXCL   0x400   /* not used by bin_io */
#endif  /* FCNTL_H */
```

[LOCAL NOTES]

117

NAME
    5.1_compilers - avoiding non-portable compiler features

STANDARD
    Portable programs should avoid compiler-dependent features.

JUSTIFICATION
    The choice of compilers used for a product will be based on global issues such as license arrangements, reliability of generated code, and variety of target machines. Such choice can be severely constrained by proliferation of compiler-dependent code.

ALTERNATIVES
    Some projects may see a need for compiler-dependent features. In these cases, a task force should plan for the possible migration to other compilers, and devise a method for porting the programs to these other compilers.

[LOCAL NOTES]

[LOCAL NOTES]

NAME
5.2_comments - suggested use of comments

GUIDELINE
A function which performs a simple transformation on its arguments may adequately be documented by a one-line "verb + objects" header comment. For larger or more complicated functions, a good explanatory comment should describe the important data structures used and should depict the control flow with a few lines of "pseudo-code" or "program design language".

Ideally, the use of meaningful variable names and clear control structures will eliminate the need for line-by-line commenting, but each "paragraph" or logical grouping of statements will be made more readable by a comment prior to the block, indented at the same level as the statements.

Where an individual statement needs clarification (even after attempts to clarify the code itself), its explanatory comment is placed at the right of the line being explained. This form of comment is also useful for describing declarations.

A related guideline for other variable declarations is that a declaration which specifies an initial value will declare only one variable, and a comment can conveniently be placed at the right of the line.

Modifications made after the initial release of a product should be documented by a similar comment on the right of the line, formatted in a standard way. A related recommended practice is for each subproject to keep a numbered log of change-requirements, and to refer to the appropriate number in the comment.

Use # if 0 if there is a need to comment-out sections of code. (RDS 1.6) Comments do not nest, in Standard C.

JUSTIFICATION
Following the style of examples shown in programming textbooks usually gives insufficient clues about what the function does; this is because textbooks actually contain the "comments" in the text of the book.

One good practical test of the amount of commenting needed is this: "Can the reviewer understand the function without detailed coaching from the author?".

It must be recognized that there is such a thing as over-commenting, which restates the obvious and slows down comprehension by sheer weight of reading matter. Therefore, individual judgement is needed.

EXAMPLE

One function from a larger file:

```
static ITEM *phead = NULL;  /* head of singly-linked list */
/*
 * cbsave - save a composite-bill item on list
 *
 *  look for the identifier s on the list
 *  if found
 *      increment its quantity field
 *  else
 *      allocate a new item
 *      splice it into the list
 */
void cbsave(
    char s[],      /* identifier field of a cb item */
    int n)         /* quantity field of a cb item */
    {
    ITEM *p, *q;    /* pointers to current item */
    ITEM **from;    /* address of the link that points to p */

    for (from = &phead, p = phead;
        p && strcmp(s, p->part_no) > 0;
         from = &p->next, p = p->next)
        ;
    if (p && strcmp(s, p->part_no) == 0) /* Rel 1.1 mod 7 */
        p->qty += n;
    else
        {
        q = malloc(sizeof(ITEM));
        q->next = p, p = q;
        p->qty = n;
        strfit(p->part_no, s, sizeof(p->part_no));
        *from = p;
        }
    }
```

[LOCAL NOTES]

NAME
     5.3_specs - specifications

STANDARD
     A program must be unmistakably matched to an external specifica-
     tion (such as a library manual page, like this page).

     The program must meet all the demands of its specification (sum-
     marizable as "the program must work").

     If a program consists of multiple source files, there must be a visi-
     ble way to tell what files these are (since its specification applies to
     the entire set). On UNIX systems, one standard way to show the
     correspondence is in the "Makefile" which shows the command
     which compiles the main function. For example, the command

```
cc -o mainpgm mainpgm.o file2.o file3.o
```

     shows the three files involved.

JUSTIFICATION
     That the program works correctly is the fundamental criterion.

     Verifying its correctness requires a specification to check it against.

[LOCAL NOTES]

[LOCAL NOTES]

NAME
5.4_reviews - code reviews

STANDARD
If a program is to be part of a released product, the program must be reviewed by one or more people other than its author.

The names of author and reviewer(s) must be documented in a comment.

The reviewer's concurrence means "I have read all the code and its corresponding specification. As best I can tell, the program is understandable, meets its specification, and conforms to all applicable standards. I would be able to maintain it."

Requisite efficiency may be considered a part of the specification, and should be spelled out explicitly in critical cases.

The review process applies to the entire source file, rather than to each function separately; the source file is the basic entity for software administration.

Each project whose management supports the resources for *correct, reliable code* will conduct some form of structured code reviews, such as "first-order correctness reviews":

> **First-order correctness review:** A review that produces a hardcopy list of test cases that would be needed in order to bracket all boundary values and to test all distinct cases (of both program and specification). (Testing "all distinct cases" guarantees "branch coverage" — all Boolean results are made to be *true* by some test case, and *false* by some other test case.)

The report from a first-order correctness review can conveniently be used for subsequent *first-order correctness testing*, which produces an automated regression test.

JUSTIFICATION
There is a class of bugs known as "blind spots" which will never be found by the author. This means that all applications that require *correctness* in the product must have some procedure for review by someone other than the author.

It is desirable to have a procedure such as "code review" or "walkthrough" which formalizes the review process, but even without formal processes, the interests of future maintainers demand that the program must be understandable by someone other than its original author.

For more details about first-order testing, refer to *Learning to Program in C*, Chapter 6, or 7.1_review in this manual.

[LOCAL NOTES]

NAME
5.5_defensive - defensive programming

STANDARD

Programs should not "blow up" or behave unpredictably in the face of out-of-bounds data (including I/O problems like "out of space"). This does not mean that programs are required to explicitly *diagnose* every out-of-bounds condition — only that they should behave sensibly. Nor does it mean that every *function* is required to perform bounds-checking. Somewhere within the *source file* must be found the code that will protect against out-of-bounds data.

Regarding the I/O library functions, two methods are acceptable:

1. Check every returned value from each function which provides error information. (Simply casting the function call to (void) is worse than nothing in this regard, and is to be avoided.)

2. Test the error status of each file, using ferror, as often as desired. Before closing the file, flush its last buffer before the final ferror test:

    ```
    /* all finished with file fp */
    fflush(fp);
    if (ferror(fp))
        /* handle the error situation */
    fclose(fp);
    ```

JUSTIFICATION

Specifications should not be burdened with case-by-case requirements that programs behave sensibly; this should be assumed as a quality of professional software.

On the other hand, requiring bounds-checking on every statement or even every function can be grossly inefficient. The choice of the *source file* as the locus of responsibility is predicated on the choice made in 5.4_reviews that the source file is the basic entity for software review and administration.

As described in 0.1_standards, exceptions must be noted in comments.

[LOCAL NOTES]

[LOCAL NOTES]

NAME
　　5.6_simplicity - simplicity of design and implementation

GUIDELINE
　　Keep it simple.

　　Needless complexity contributes to unreliability.

　　Estimate in advance the necessary areas of generality, then meet them. Do not generalize everything.

　　Estimate in advance the likely future requirements of portability, then meet them. Do not attempt portability to any and all conceivable future environments, unless that is an agreed-upon requirement of the project.

　　Before designing dynamic data structures, consider whether a simple array will work, or a dynamically-allocated array that is occasionally re-sized with `realloc`.

[LOCAL NOTES]

[LOCAL NOTES]

NAME
   6.1_stdc - features of Standard C

This chapter will present a detailed list of the ways that C has changed since its 1978 presentation in Kernighan and Ritchie (K&R). The list omits many clarifications that are of interest primarily to compiler writers. It is arranged in roughly the same topic sequence as the K&R Appendix A, which is more or less the sequence of the C Standard.

To begin with, there are some precise definitions of basic terms.

The Standard allows interactive interpreters as well as traditional compilers, and uses the more universal term "translator" to apply to both. (However, in these notes, "compiler" includes interpreters too.)

An "undefined behavior" results from an erroneous or non-portable construct; the compiler is not obliged to diagnose it, although good-quality compilers will diagnose many of them. Arithmetic overflow during expression evaluation is an example of an undefined behavior.

An "implementation-defined behavior" is one where compilers have some latitude among several choices, but the choice must be documented in the compiler manual. An obvious example is the number of bytes in each multi-byte data type.

A "syntax rule" is a context-free-grammar rule of the language. Compilers are obliged to produce diagnostic messages for violations of syntax rules.

A "constraint" is a context-sensitive restriction imposed upon the syntax. For example, the multiplication operator requires that both operands have arithmetic type (i.e., integer or floating). Compilers are obliged to produce diagnostic messages for violations of constraints.

An "object" is a region of storage which can contain data values. In other words, an object is a variable or a region of the (data) storage which can be accessed through a pointer.

The term "lvalue" is essentially equivalent to "a variable name, or an expression that can be used like a variable name". This is more of a clarification than a change. Some lvalues are "modifiable" (such as ordinary variables), and others are not (such as arrays and const variables). Only the modifiable lvalues can be assigned into, incremented, or decremented.

The encoding of integers must be binary (i.e., base-2 numbers). (This implies that bitwise operations upon non-negative integers can be used in portable programs.)

Certain environmental aspects are *locale-specific* and vary with nationality, culture, and language: target character set, implementation-defined aspects of <ctype.h> functions, collating sequence, the "decimal indicator character" (period or comma), and certain time-and-date formats. The output of a strictly conforming program is allowed to depend upon locale-specific characteristics, but not upon other implementation-defined characteristics. One implication, for a simple example, is that a strictly conforming ("maximally portable") program may produce ASCII output in one environment and EBCDIC output in another.

A conforming implementation may have extensions (including additional library functions), *provided that* they do not alter the behavior of a strictly conforming program. The "provided that" protects the writer of ostensibly-portable programs from rude shocks like discovering that a variable name such as err01a (say) conflicts with a "magic" reserved word in some new implementation.

Therefore, the Standard Libraries that come with a compiler can only call upon other Standard functions or functions with a "leading-underscore" name. Each particular implementation is also likely to support a (non-Standard) library that provides access to implementation-specific functions (typically without the leading-underscore name).

[LOCAL NOTES]

NAME
    6.2_environ - environment of Standard C

Let us define a *strictly portable* program as one which must produce identical behavior in any Standard C environment. (The Standard refers to a "strictly conforming" program, but the word "portable" is more accurately intuitive.) This means, for example, that a strictly portable program cannot depend upon the specific int size of the processor or the specific internal representation of floating-point numbers. Certain minimal guarantees are given, however: int's have at least 16 bits, and float's can hold at least 6 digits of precision.

A strictly portable program should not produce or use any values that are outside these ranges:

char	0 to 127
unsigned char	0 to 255
short	-32,767 *[yes]* to 32,767
unsigned short	0 to 65,535
long	-2,147,483,647 to 2,147,483,647
unsigned long	0 to 4,294,967,295
float exponent	-38 to 38
float precision	6 decimal digits

A strictly portable program should not contain more than ...

6 significant characters in an external identifier
8 nesting levels of #if, or of #include
12 *, [], or () modifiers on one declarator
15 nesting levels of control structure
31 arguments on one macro invocation, or on one function call
31 significant characters in an internal identifier
31 parentheses nesting in one declaration, or in one expression
127 local identifiers in one block
127 expressions nested with parentheses
127 constants in one enum declaration
127 members in one structure or union
257 case labels in one switch
509 characters on one source line, or in one string constant
511 external identifiers in one source file
1024 macro names in one source file
32767 bytes in one declared object

A program might exceed one or more of these limits and still be "widely portable", but it will probably fail somewhere, sometime. (This is just to re-emphasize the meaning of "strictly portable".)

Adding the word "non-portable" to the definition of "undefined behavior" was meant to more clearly convey the committee's intent regarding the impact of the Standard. As always, a "strictly conforming" program is one which is highly portable. The restrictions given in the Standard apply only to these "strictly conforming" programs. In the future, just as now, there will also be a large population of C programs which are not intended to be universally portable; these are the programs written for a specific machine and/or a specific operating system.

Committee members have occasionally heard complaints from the public to the effect that "X3J11 has *broken* my programs with your decisions about . . ." (macros, or the signal function, or whatever). In most such cases, the standard has simply labeled these as "undefined behaviors", meaning that they are not allowed in a strictly conforming ("strictly portable") program. They were, in fact, never portable constructs; they just happen to work in the particular environment that they were programmed for. Typically, nothing has really changed; the categories of conformance have just been made more precise and more explicit.

The Standard specifies the exact sequencing of comment-replacement, tokenizing, preprocessing, and syntax analysis. After the original source-file line numbers are noted, comments are replaced by one blank.

A hosted environment calls main with arguments, and provides the full Standard Library. A freestanding environment may have its own non-standard library.

Numerical limits for float, double, and long double are provided in <float.h>. The header <limits.h> specifies ranges for integer data. The headers <float.h>, <limits.h>, <stddef.h>, and <stdarg.h> are required in both hosted and freestanding environments.

Implementers are urged to avoid "hard translation limits". In other words, if a compiler is confronted with a very large program, and the compiler can obtain extra memory for its tables, it should use the extra memory.

A compiler must be capable of compiling at least one program which meets or exceeds all specified translation limits. Thus, a "toy" compiler whose symbol table is limited to 32 identifiers is not a conforming implementation.

Some of the C source characters do not appear in some European versions of the ASCII character set. To allow the representation of C programs in the widest range of source character sets, a standard set of mappings is provided. Each time that one of these three-character "trigraphs" appears, it is replaced (in the first phase of compilation) by its corresponding C source character:

```
??=   #
??(   [
??)   ]
??/   \
??'   ^
??<   {
??>   }
??!   |
??-   ~
```

This mapping is *always* performed, so the string `"What??!"` would become `"What|"`. A uniform method of preventing this confusion in existing programs is to insert a backslash between any sequence of two question-marks (as in `"What?\?!"`).

Two new character escape sequences are defined: `\a` ("alarm") produces "bell", and `\v` produces vertical tab. (An escape sequence such as `\e` was repeatedly suggested for the ASCII "escape" code ESC, but the semantics are non-portable and ESC does not exist in some popular character sets such as EBCDIC.)

Identifiers starting with one underscore are (in principle) reserved, except for non-external identifiers starting with underscore followed by a lower-case letter (e.g. for user-defined "hidden" member names).

A cross-compiler must give the same results as a native compiler, except for preprocessor `#if` arithmetic, which is allowed to use the arithmetic of a cross-compiler host.

[LOCAL NOTES]

[LOCAL NOTES]

NAME

   6.3_language - language features of Standard C

Vertical tab and form feed are whitespace source characters, as are the more familiar space, tab, newline, and comment. Any line ending in backslash gets the following line spliced on.

The entry keyword is out. Several new keywords have become reserved words: const, enum, signed, void, and volatile. Further discussion of each new keyword appears later in this section.

Identifiers are in principle limited only by logical line length, but at least 31 characters are significant for non-external identifiers.

Later re-declarations of external names can add information to the type: array sizes can be added later, and structure-or-union types can be completed. Thus, this fragment is allowable:

```
int a[];
struct b;
int a[5] = {0};
struct b {float r, i;};
```

The scope of an identifier extends from the end of its declarator. This allows, for example, the use of the identifier in its own initializer:

```
struct loop {struct loop *p; short data;} head = {&head, 0};
```

Names declared with extern storage class have the same lexical scope (block or file) as other names; reference to an out-of-scope name produces undefined behavior.

Linkage rules are slightly more permissive than K&R. UNIX-style "common" linkage becomes non-standard, but may be provided as an extension.

Member names in different structures had to be distinct in K&R; now each structure (or union) has its own member name space.

These are the name space categories: ordinary identifiers, labels, and tags. Each structure or union also has its own member name space. Here is an artificial but valid example:

```
void abc()
    {
    struct abc {char abc;};
    goto abc;
    abc: return;
    }
```

A function returning nothing has void type. The integer types (char, short, int, and long) accept the modifiers signed and unsigned. A long double may be larger than double. In C environments that use the IEEE floating-point representation, long double can designate the 80-bit "extended" precision.

The old form long float is an invalid type combination; it is no longer a synonym for double.

The Standard introduces the term "compatible" for two types which can be used to designate the same object or function; the term "compatible" means "exactly the same, or close enough". For example, types named by typedef are compatible with their underlying type, and therefore this code sequence —

```
extern int a[];
typedef int INT;
extern INT a[];
```
— is valid (although rather silly).

Even if two types (short, int, or long) have the same representation, they are still different types, and hence not compatible. This means, among other things, that a pointer-to-short cannot be assigned to a pointer-to-int without using a cast. Ditto for float, double, and long double.

Arithmetic involving unsigned types cannot overflow, because it involves a "modulo" arithmetic.

Floating constants may have the suffix L (or l) for long double, or the suffix F (or f) for float.

The digits 8 and 9 are not valid in octal contexts. The digits 0 through 9 are guaranteed to be contiguous codes.

Integer constants may have the suffix U (or u) for unsigned (possibly combined with "long" suffix, as in 123456UL).

If the high-order bit of an octal or hex int constant is 1, the type of the constant is unsigned int. Thus, the type of 0x7FFF is int, but the type of 0xFFFF is unsigned int (in 16-bit environments). If the high-order bit of any long constant is 1, the type of the constant is unsigned long. Thus, the type of 2000000000 is long, but the type of 4000000000 is unsigned long (if long is 32 bits).

If char is signed, the high bit of a single-character constant is treated as a sign bit.

137

Hexadecimal character constants have the form `'\xFF'`, with no lexical limit upon the number of digits.

Adjacent "unit string literals" catenate:

```
"hel" "lo"      produces      "hello"
"\x12""3"       produces      "\x12" catenated with "3"
```

The type of a string literal is simply "array of `char`". Strings are nonetheless semantically intended to be non-modifiable, and the compiler may put them into write-protected memory or into ROM. Instances of identical strings might or might not be given distinct storage.

"A `char`, `signed char`, `unsigned char`, `short int`, or `unsigned short int` may be used in an expression wherever an `int` may be used. In all cases the value is converted to an `int` if an `int` can represent all values of the original type, otherwise it is converted to `unsigned int`. These are called the integral promotions." This approach to the promotion of small unsigned numbers is known as the "value-preserving" rule. Of course, in K&R there were no `unsigned char` or `unsigned short` types, so their promotions were not specified. Since then, UNIX compilers have chosen to promote them to `unsigned int` in all environments — the so-called "unsignedness-preserving" rule. The committee adopted the value-preserving rule largely because of well-known portability problems with the unsignedness-preserving rules. The change is unlikely to affect any already-portable code; the entire source code for UNIX has been successfully ported using a compiler with value-preserving promotions.

Floating-to-integer conversion always truncates toward zero, even for negative values.

Conversion of a longer floating type to a shorter floating type produces either rounding or chopping, implementation-defined.

In the "usual arithmetic conversions", if either operand is `long double`, the operation and result are `long double`. If neither operand is as wide as `double`, and one operand is `float`, then the result is `float`. In other words, `float` is an acceptable "intermediate" type, just as `double` has always been.

Operands may be promoted to other (wider) types, provided neither range nor precision is lost. (This allows, for example, certain floating-point processors to do all operations in extended precision.)

A pointer to any object type may be converted to a "generic" pointer and back again without change. The syntax for generic pointer is now `void *`. The same internal representation is used for `void *` and `char *`.

The integer constant value zero (0) may be assigned to a pointer (producing a *null pointer*) or compared for equality with a pointer.

A generic pointer may not be the operand of indirection operations (* []
->), pointer arithmetic operations (+ -), or relational operations (< <= >
>=).

If pfn is of type "pointer to function", the expression pfn() means the same as (*pfn)().

Structures and unions may be assigned, passed as function arguments, and returned from functions, provided that source and destination are of the same type.

Old-style assignment operators (=+) are out.

If the left operand of assignment is a pointer, the right operand must have compatible type, or be a generic pointer, or be a null pointer constant.

The address-of operator (&) may be applied to a function (which returns some type); the resulting type is "pointer to function returning that type". Address-of may also be applied to an array of arbitrary type; the resulting type is "pointer to array of that type".

Unary plus (+) is defined.

Expression grouping (as specified by left-to-right association and by parentheses) is always honored; in the expression a + (b + c), b and c will be added together before a is added to their sum.

The type produced by the sizeof operator is implementation-defined, either unsigned int or unsigned long. The appropriate type is provided in <stddef.h> as size_t. (<stddef.h> is required in both hosted and freestanding environments.)

sizeof(char) equals 1.

It is no longer guaranteed that an int or even a long int is large enough to hold a pointer. (See "Generic pointer", above.)

In pointer arithmetic, a location within an array can be meaningfully compared to or subtracted from the first location past the array. Aside from this special case, the behavior is undefined when one location is inside an array and the other location is outside that array.

The restrictions upon constant expressions are stated more precisely. A very rough generalization is that each category of constant expression allows just those expressions that a compiler can be guaranteed to be able to compute at compile time. The comma operator is disallowed in constant expressions. For example,

```
int a[1,10];
```

becomes a syntax error instead of a puzzle.

Old-style initializers without equal-sign are out.

A strictly portable program must not contain "vacuuous declarations". That is, every declaration must contain an identifier — either a declarator, or an enumeration named constant, or a tag name. This means that vacuous declarations like

```
int ;
```

are now invalid.

A bit field declared as int may be treated as being either signed int or unsigned int, implementation-defined.

The storage boundary for bit fields is implementation-defined. (Previously, it was required to be int.) Whether a field can straddle the boundary is also implementation-defined. This allows implementers more latitude in being able to support bit fields more efficiently if they wish.

A structure (or union) tag declaration with no declarator such as

```
struct abc;
```

refers (either forward or backward) to another declaration in the same block (to hide any outer declaration).

Enumeration types are provided, essentially as introduced in UNIX 7th Edition (1979). They still do not provide any stricter type-checking than would be available from simple #define's. For example,

```
enum stoplight {RED, YELLOW, GREEN};
```

provides no more type-checking than would be given by

```
#define enum_stoplight int
#define RED    0
#define YELLOW 1
#define GREEN  2
```

Using the enumeration takes fewer source lines and may produce real identifiers in the object-code symbol table. Compilers are free to use a data type smaller than int, if the range of values permits. (Some compilers, upon special request, will treat enumerations with a stricter Pascal-like type-checking, but this is non-standard.)

An object with const storage cannot be assigned to, incremented, or decremented. Thus, a declaration like

```
static const char table[][10] =
    {
    "message-1",
    /* ... */
    "message-n",
    };
static const short n_msgs = sizeof(table) / sizeof(table[0]);
```

would allow a compiler to put table and n_msgs into a ROM segment or a memory-protected segment. Any occurrence of ++n_msgs (for example) would produce a syntax error. To help prevent modification of const data via pointers, a pointer-to-const cannot be assigned to a pointer-to-non-const (unless an explicit cast is used). Consider the pointer declaration

```
const char *format;
```

This says that format is a pointer to const char's. Such pointers are "in-only" pointers; they can be used to access data but not to modify it.

References to an object with volatile storage cannot be "optimized away". All operations upon such objects must produce actual fetch or store operations, in accordance with the "abstract machine" semantics. A pointer-to-volatile cannot be assigned to a pointer-to-non-volatile.

Function declarations with parameter declaration lists are called *proto-types*:

```
extern double sqrt(double);
```

says that sqrt takes a double parameter. When this prototype is visible, an argument to sqrt must be assignable to double, and will be converted (as if by assignment) to double. Any call to sqrt with the wrong number of arguments (such as sqrt(2, 0)) will be diagnosed as a syntax error.

```
extern int getchar(void);
```

says explicitly that getchar has no parameter.

```
extern FILE *fopen();
```

is not a prototype; it has no parameter information. It is still allowed for compatibility with existing programs.

```
extern FILE *fopen(const char *fname, const char *mode);
```

uses the dummy parameter names fname and mode. The names go out of scope at the end of the prototype, and are for documentation purposes only.

```
extern int printf(const char *fmt, ...);
```

has an "ellipsis" in the parameter list, indicating that zero or more (unchecked) arguments may follow, providing a "variable argument-list" syntax.

The keyword register will be allowed (and ignored) in prototype parameter declarations.

Structures, union, and enumeration types declared in separate files are compatible if they have the same member names, the same number of members, and compatible member types. For two structures, the members must be in the same order; for two enumerations, the members must have the same values.

Automatic aggregates can be initialized. Initializers for automatic aggregates must contain constant expressions. This means that they have the same syntax as initializers for static aggregates.

Unions can be initialized, through the member that appears first in the declaration of the union:

```
union ic {short i; char c;} ic1 = {0xFFFF};
```

initializes ic1.i.

The switch expression may be any integer type, including long and unsigned long.

Labels have "function scope". Therefore, goto can jump into the middle of a block. (This is not a recommended practice.) Any associated block-level initializer would be skipped.

A return'ed expression must be assignment-compatible with the declared return-type.

A function parameter cannot be re-declared as an auto. This prevents a common bug:

```
void f(i)
    int i;
    {
    /* ... */
    int i;     /* now a syntax error */
```

If a prototype is visible when a function is defined, and the prototype has an "ellipsis" or specifies a non-default parameter type, the same prototype is required to be visible anywhere the function is called. Thus, a prototype may allow faster argument passing for non-default sizes, such as char, short, and float. The old default argument-promotion rules (int, long, double) apply only when no prototype is visible, or when ellipsis terminates the prototype, or when the prototype specifies nothing but default sizes.

A function may be defined with the same syntax as used in prototypes; for example,

```
void plot(double x, double y)
    {
    /* ... */
    }
```

To follow existing conventions for layout and commenting of function definitions, the preceding could be re-written:

```
void plot(
    double x,    /* comment describing x */
    double y)    /* comment describing y */
    {
    /* ... */
    }
```

This serves both as prototype and as definition. This syntax is known as the "new-style" function definition syntax; the Standard deprecates the previous "old style". If the new style becomes sufficiently widespread in the next few years, a future C Standard could eliminate support for the old style.

External data definition rules accept most existing varieties of C, except for UNIX "common" linkage rules, which may be provided as an extension.

[LOCAL NOTES]

NAME
    6.4_pp - preprocessor for Standard C

Tabs and blanks (including blanks produced by comments) may precede or follow the # that begins a preprocessing directive.

The preprocessor grammar is rather precisely specified in syntax notation, in a fashion that allows preprocessing to be done before or after tokenization.

Besides the two usual forms

```
#include "header1"
#include <header2>
```

the new form

```
#include header3
```

is allowed (if header3 is a macro name which evaluates to one of the other forms).

File names specified by #include are searched first in the "directory" of the top level source file.

A macro may be #define'd several times, provided that all definitions are tokenwise identical (known as "benign re-definition"). Thus, each header can state what it understands the definition to be, and if the understandings differ, the compiler will complain.

A macro name appearing during the expansion of its own definition is not re-expanded, allowing definitions like

```
#define open(fd, m)  open(fd, m|NEW_MODE, 0)
```

The precise behavior is as follows: A macro name is temporarily #undef'ed during scanning of its replacement (preventing endless expansion of recursions). Furthermore, each occurrence of an #undef'ed name in a replacement is marked ("painted blue") to prevent it from being expanded in any later scanning. Arguments to macros-with-parameters are scanned and expanded before insertion into the replacement. Rescanning of the replacement can require further input text (on the right-hand end).

These rules allow, for example, the passing of the name of a macro as an argument to another macro:


```
#define add(x, y) (x + y)
#define binop(op, a, b) op(a, b)

binop(add, c, d)
```

which produces `(c + d)`.

For an example involving "marking" of replacements, consider this admittedly-contrived excerpt:

```
#define f(x) (f(x) != 0)
#define g(a) ((a) + EPS)
#define EPS  1

n = g(f(2));
```

Using the notation `@f` to indicate the symbol `f` marked for non-replacement ("painted blue"), the expansion proceeds like this:

```
g(f(2))
    f(2)
    (@f(2) != 0)
g((@f(2) != 0))
(((@f(2) != 0)) + EPS)
(((@f(2) != 0)) + 1)
```

After all scanning and replacement is complete, removing the "blue paint" marks produces

```
n = (((f(2) != 0)) + 1);
```

The draft is now much closer to the behavior of the UNIX preprocessor in certain cases where a macro replacement builds an invocation of another macro. (Whether such practices should be discouraged as hard-to-read is a separate question.)

In a macro definition, an appearance of

> *token* ## *token*

causes the two tokens to be catenated lexically, thus forming one token. If a catenated token is a macro formal parameter, the (unexpanded) actual argument is used. Otherwise, the unexpanded token itself is used. For example:

```
#define NXCAT(a, b) a ## b   /* catenate a and b with no expansion */
#define CAT(a, b) NXCAT(a, b)  /* expand a and b, then catenate */

#define PKG graph

    CAT(open, PKG)(x)
```

produces

```
opengraph(x)
```

This is equivalent to the (pre-1989) UNIX preprocessor's behavior for a definition such as

```
#define NXCAT(a, b)  a/**/b
```

Catenation is done early in macro expansion. There is no separate phase of translation for catenation; catenation is part of macro expansion.

In the replacement string of a macro definition, an appearance of

> # *identifier*

produces the "string-ization" of the identifier. For example,

```
#define PR(x) printf(#x " = %d\n", x)
PR(nc);
```

produces

```
printf("nc" " = %d\n", nc);
```

which, after string-literal catenation, becomes

```
printf("nc = %d\n", nc);
```

The macro names ___LINE___ and ___FILE___ are pre-defined (as in UNIX 7th Edition), and expand into the current line number and the current file name.

A new directive, #elif, ("else if") is allowed after the #if varieties. The macro expressions

```
defined identifier
defined ( identifier )
```

may be tested on a #if line; thus,

```
#if defined(BUFSIZ)
    /* ... */
#elif defined(NULL)
    /* ... */
#endif
```

is equivalent to

```
#ifdef BUFSIZ
   /* ... */
#else
#ifdef NULL
   /* ... */
#endif
#endif
```

Invoking a macro-with-parameters with an empty argument produces an undefined result. For example,

```
#define x(a) fnx(a)

n = x();
```

is not a strictly-conforming Standard C program. The compiler can diagnose it and disallow it, or it can accept it, thus generating a call to fnx(). The program can be considered either "non-portable" or "erroneous", depending upon your point of view.

The builtin macro __DATE__ produces a string like "Jan 21 1987". Similarly, __TIME__ produces a string like "16:45:30".

A line of the form

```
#pragma anything-but-newline   newline
```

causes (non-standardized) implementation-defined special behavior.

A line containing no tokens except one # is allowed and ignored.

The macro name __STDC__ will be pre-defined (equal to 1) in a conforming implementation.

The identifiers defined, __FILE__, __LINE__, __TIME__, __DATE__, and __STDC__ may not be #define'd or #undef'ed.

#error *stuff* will produce a diagnostic containing *stuff*.

[LOCAL NOTES]

NAME
     6.5_library - library of Standard C

The library names are (in principle) reserved names. If you write your own version of fopen, say, your program *might* work in some environment that you know well, but it would have slim chances of being generally portable.

Each library function is declared in one of the Standard header files, and described in one of the next twelve sections:

6.6_general	<limits.h>	Integer parameters
	<float.h>	Floating-point parameters
	<stddef.h>	Common definitions
	<errno.h>	Errors
6.7_assert	<assert.h>	Diagnostics
6.8_ctype	<ctype.h>	Character handling
6.9_locale	<locale.h>	Internationalization
6.10_math	<math.h>	Mathematics
6.11_setjmp	<setjmp.h>	Non-local jumps
6.12_signal	<signal.h>	Signal handling
6.13_stdarg	<stdarg.h>	Variable-length argument lists
6.14_stdio	<stdio.h>	Input/output
6.15_stdlib	<stdlib.h>	General utilities
6.16_string	<string.h>	String handling
6.17_time	<time.h>	Date and time

Any function may be implemented as a "protected" #define macro, i.e. one which evaluates each argument exactly once. But each function must also be present in callable form in the library, so that

     #undef *function-name*

guarantees a real function (to take its address, find it in a "profile", set a breakpoint, etc.).

Except for internal names starting with underscore and a lower-case letter, no names beginning with underscore can be used in a strictly portable program. They are available for use by the implementer for "hidden" macros. On the other hand, among the names that do not start with underscore, implementers can use only those that appear in the Standard. The intent is to allow the possibility of strictly portable programs that do not "trip over" into the names used by the implementers.

A strictly portable program must #include <stdio.h> before calling any of the printf or scanf functions, because these functions may need special calling sequences to access variable-length argument lists.

The following sections list all the library functions of Standard C, grouped in their appropriate headers. These descriptions are not meant to convey every detail from the Standard, or to replace your vendor's reference manual; instead, they are concise summaries intended to convey the essential features of the functions. Primary emphasis is given to new functionality, new features, and other differences.

[LOCAL NOTES]

NAME
6.6_general - basic headers: `<limits.h>`, `<float.h>`, `<stddef.h>`, `<errno.h>`

`<limits.h>` -- Sizes of integral types

This header contains definitions for the limiting values for the various integral types. Each definition produces a constant expression suitable for use in `#if` preprocessing directives.

CHAR_BIT   the number of bits in a `char`.

SCHAR_MIN   the minimum value of a `signed char`.

SCHAR_MAX   the maximum value of a `signed char`.

CHAR_MIN   the minimum value of a `char`.

CHAR_MAX   the maximum value of a `char`.

UCHAR_MAX   the maximum value of an `unsigned char`.

SHRT_MIN   the minimum value of a `short`.

SHRT_MAX   the maximum value of a `short`.

USHRT_MAX   the maximum value of an `unsigned short`.

INT_MIN   the minimum value of a `int`.

INT_MAX   the maximum value of a `int`.

UINT_MAX   the maximum value of an `unsigned int`.

LONG_MIN   the minimum value of a `long`.

LONG_MAX   the maximum value of a `long`.

ULONG_MAX   the maximum value of an `unsigned long`.

MB_LEN_MAX   maximum length of a "multibyte" (international) character

`<float.h>` -- Characteristics of floating types

This header describes floating-point representations in terms of a specified mathematical model. It is primarily of importance to numerical analysts and other floating-point programmers, and will not be detailed here.

<stddef.h> -- Common definitions

These definitions are important for writing portable code.

ptrdiff_t

> The signed integral type of the result of subtracting two pointers. (It is usually int, but in environments that support very large objects, it could be long.)

size_t

> The unsigned integral type of the result of the sizeof operator. Function parameters that accept the size of an object are declared to have the size_t type.

wchar_t

> The integral type large enough to hold a "wide character" in any supported international code set.

NULL

> Produces a null pointer constant. It could be 0, or 0L, or (void *)0, at the implementer's choice.

offsetof(structure-type, member)

> Tells the offset (in bytes) of member within the structure-type.

<errno.h> -- Errors

This header provides errno, the global error-indicator variable. Many functions in the Standard library (including math, input-output, and conversion functions) set errno to a non-zero value to indicate the occurrence of an error. Also provided are the macro values EDOM, ERANGE, and possibly other implementation-defined names.

[LOCAL NOTES]

NAME

6.7_assert - executable assertions `<assert.h>`

The macro `assert(expression)` is provided.

If the macro `NDEBUG` is *not* defined at the point that you `#include <assert.h>`, then `assert` will generate a diagnostic message, and an `abort` termination, if the `expression` is false.

[LOCAL NOTES]

[LOCAL NOTES]

NAME
6.8_ctype - character handling <ctype.h>

Some of the character-handling functions are essentially unchanged
from their descriptions in K&R: isalpha, isdigit, islower, isspace, isupper,
tolower, and toupper. With the addition of "internationalization" to C, the
<ctype.h> functions behave appropriately to the specified "locale". (See
6.9_locale below for further details.)

Here are the functions:

int isalpha(int c);

Tells whether c is an alphabetic character.

int isalnum(int c);

Tells whether c is an alphanumeric character.

int iscntrl(int c);

Tells whether c is a control character.

int isdigit(int c);

Tells whether c is a digit character.

int isgraph(int c);

Tells whether c is a printing character (other than space).

int islower(int c);

Tells whether c is a lower-case letter.

int isprint(int c);

Tells whether c is a printing character.

int ispunct(int c);

Tells whether c is a punctuation character.

int isspace(int c);

Tells whether c is a whitespace character.

int isupper(int c);

Tells whether c is an upper-case letter.

int isxdigit(int c);

Tells whether c is a hexadecimal-digit character.

```
int tolower(int c);
```

> If c is an upper-case letter, converts c into a lower-case letter; otherwise, just returns c.

```
int toupper(int c);
```

> If c is a lower-case letter, converts c into an upper-case letter; otherwise, just returns c.

[LOCAL NOTES]

NAME
6.9_locale - international localization `<locale.h>`

A new header has been added for internationalization, `<locale.h>`. There are several named constants that designate different aspects of the locale:

`LC_ALL`   designates all locale-specific characteristics.

`LC_COLLATE`   designates the collating sequence.

`LC_CTYPE`   designates the `<ctype.h>` characteristics.

`LC_MONETARY`   designates monetary formatting characteristics.

`LC_NUMERIC`   designates the decimal indicator character.

`LC_TIME`   designates some time-and-date formats.

Two functions are declared in this header:

`char *setlocale(int category, const char *locale);`

> can be used to change locale-specific characteristics, and to inquire about their current settings. If the `locale` string is `"C"`, the (English) minimal environment for C is specified. If `locale` is `""`, the implementation-defined native environment is specified (which can be the same as `"C"`). Other implementation-defined strings (typically accessed through the `getenv` environment) can also be specified. If `locale` is a null pointer, the `setlocale` function returns the current locale string associated with the specified `category`.

> At program startup, the equivalent of `setlocale(LC_ALL, "C")` is executed. If you want your program to adapt to the implementation-defined native environment, then execute `setlocale(LC_ALL, "")` early in the program.

`const struct lconv *localeconv(void);`

> returns a pointer to a structure containing information about the formatting of monetary and non-monetary quantities.

To allow a program to adapt to different collating sequences, two functions (`strcoll` and `strxfrm`) are provided in `<string.h>`:

`int strcoll(const char *s1, const char *s2);`

> behaves just like the familiar `strcmp`, except that the current locale-specific collating sequence is used for comparisons.

```
size_t strxfrm(char *to, const char *from, size_t maxsize);
```
This will create a "sorting key" in the first `maxsize` characters of the `to` string, such that when compared with another sorting key (using `strcmp` or `memcmp`), the comparison will reflect the (current) collating sequence. The returned value indicates the length of the required result, which could be even larger than twice the length of the `from` string. If `maxsize` is too small for this result, the `to` string has unspecified contents.

To allow the printing of dates and times in a locale-specific format, the `strftime` function is provided:

```
size_t strftime(char *s, size_t maxsize, const char *format, const struct tm *tp);
```
The `format` string is similar to a `printf` format string; it can contain constant text to be printed as-is, along with percent-sign directives. The directives produce various output-string representations of the time and date information in the `*tp` structure:

```
%a  abbreviated weekday name
%A  full weekday name
%b  abbreviated month name
%B  full month name
%c  appropriate date and time
    ... (etc.) ...
%Z  timezone name (if available)
```

When the locale is changed (using a `setlocale` call that specifies either `LC_ALL` or `LC_TIME`) subsequent calls to `strftime` will use language and format appropriate to the new locale.

The existing time-and-date functions (`asctime` and `ctime`) produce a specific (English) format, as before. Thus, these two sequences produce essentially the same string result:

```
/* #1: produce English date+time */
strcpy(str, asctime(&my_tm));

/* #2: produce English date+time */
setlocale(LC_TIME, "C"); /* if needed */
strftime(str, sizeof(str), "%c\n", &my_tm);
```

The numeric input, output, and conversion functions in `<stdio.h>` and `<stdlib.h>` use the decimal indicator character specified by the current locale, as set by a `setlocale` call for `LC_ALL` or `LC_NUMERIC`.

The `LC_CTYPE` locale governs the behavior of the `<ctype.h>` functions. In the `"C"` locale, these functions are fully specified, with no implementation-defined variations: `isalnum`, `isalpha`, `isdigit`, `isxdigit`, `isupper`, `islower`, `toupper`, and `tolower`. In the `""` ("native") locale, everything but `isdigit` and `isxdigit` is locale-specific.

GENERAL DISCUSSION

Before 1980, changing the "locale" of a program (e.g., producing a French version of a USA product) was most often accomplished by ad-hoc rewriting by hand. Few system-level facilities were available for assistance. More recently, system-level assistance was introduced by several software suppliers, but these solutions were independently developed and incompatible.

The need for standards was clear to those who were actively involved with the problem. In particular, members of the ISO working group on C told X3J11 that ISO would address the issue if X3J11 did not.

On the other hand, a majority of X3J11 desired to avoid any elaborate inventions that would complicate a language whose simplicity is a major selling point. Furthermore, it would be inappropriate to simply select one among several competing approaches. A simple, portable "umbrella" was needed which could be mapped into diverse vendor-specific approaches.

The conceptual breakthrough hinges upon the realization that most "international" programmers do not wish to have the range of target locales to be determined by the original source-code program. It is much preferable to produce a program which can adapt to its locale at system-configuration time, or even at run-time. Thus, the locale argument to setlocale is a simple character string. It could be obtained at run-time from a getenv inquiry, which could be given a default at system-configuration time, or chosen from a login menu, or specified by a login "profile".

Vendors whose markets are (currently) uninterested in these complexities can provide simple stub versions of the new functions.

Vendors in non-English markets can produce "two-locale" implementations ("native" and English) that are almost as simple.

The original USA English C locale happens to be the lowest common denominator of all the others. It is the initial default environment of any program, and it can be explicitly requested by

    setlocale(LC_ALL, "C");

For example, a programmer who desires to produce output files of the widest portability would specify the "C" locale, which specifies the minimal 26-letter alphabet, the intrinsic character-set collating sequence, and the "period" for the decimal indicator character. Since many other popular languages (e.g., Pascal) allow *only* the period, these choices are compatible with the de facto *lingua franca* of worldwide computing.

To adapt to the (implementation-defined) "local" environment, a program should specify

```
setlocale(LC_ALL, "");
```

This is the simplest way for a program to attempt being polite to its multi-national audience; it means "speak the local dialect, as best you can".

To be any more precise about the use of setlocale would involve system-dependent issues — how does a program determine the set of locally-supported locale names, how should those names appear on the screen when presented to the user, how can a user identify his or her locale as part of a "profile", etc. Each internationally-concerned system will doubtless provide answers to these questions; many already do. They are, however, just outside the scope of the C Standard.

The design of setlocale also allows a uniform direction for further extensions. For example, the run-time selection of the language for headings, error messages, etc., is an extension which is facilitated by the mechanism for setting and inquiring about the current locale.

The Standard embodies extensive support for international languages with "wide" characters. To begin with, the string literals, comments, and format strings are understood to allow "multibyte" characters, with a potentially state-dependent encoding using "shift-in" and "shift-out" codes. Such strings are still just arrays of char's, but they may require appropriate hardware to properly display the programmer's intention; for example,

```
char title[] = " <picture a Japanese (Kanji) string here> ";
```

Support is also provided for state-independent encodings, in which each wide character has its own (larger than char) integer code. The defined-type wchar_t ("wide-character type") in <stddef.h> and <stdlib.h> defines the necessary integer size (e.g., unsigned short int). Prefixing a string with an L causes the compiler to do an implementation-defined compile-time translation from the multibyte sequence of characters between the quotation-marks into an array of wchar_t integers. Thus,

```
wchar_t wtitle[] = L" <picture a Japanese (Kanji) string here> ";
```

could initialize wtitle with a sequence of wide characters, plus a terminating zero.

There are also individual wide-character constants, which look like L' <one Kanji character> '; they are integer constants of type wchar_t.

The maximum number of bytes required to represent one multibyte character, in the current locale, is given by the macro expression MB_CUR_MAX in <stdlib.h>. The largest such value, for any supported locale, is given by the macro constant MB_LEN_MAX in <limits.h>.

There are five new functions in <stdlib.h> for handling multibyte characters: wcstombs, mbstowcs, wctomb, mbtowc, and mblen. (See 6.15_stdlib for details.)

[LOCAL NOTES]

[LOCAL NOTES]

NAME

6.10_math - mathematical functions <math.h>

The mathematical functions have remained essentially unchanged since UNIX 7th Edition. Minor revisions in the Standard have served mostly to tighten and clarify, rather than to modify, their specification. The header <math.h> defines a named constant which is returned from some of the math functions when the true value is unrepresentable:

HUGE_VAL   a very large double value (possibly the IEEE "infinity")

Also defined are two named constants which are passed back in the errno global error indicator in certain erroneous situations:

EDOM   indicator of a domain error (invalid argument)

ERANGE   indicator of a range error (unrepresentable result)

```
double acos(double x);
```

Computes the arc cosine of x.

```
double asin(double x);
```

Computes the arc sine of x.

```
double atan(double x);
```

Computes the arc tangent of x.

```
double atan2(double y, double x);
```

Computes the arc tangent of y/x.

```
double ceil(double x);
```

Computes the "ceiling" of x, the smallest integer not less than x.

```
double cos(double x);
```

Computes the cosine of x.

```
double cosh(double x);
```

Computes the hyperbolic cosine of x.

```
double exp(double x);
```

Computes the exponential function of x.

```
double fabs(double x);
```

Computes the absolute value of x.

```
double floor(double x);
```

Computes the "floor" of x, the largest integer not greater than x.

```
double fmod(double x, double y);
```

Computes the floating-point remainder of x/y.

```
double frexp(double value, int *exp);
```

Computes the "fraction-and-exponent" representation of x. The returned value x lies between 0.5 and 1, and the integer *exp is set such that value equals x times 2 raised to the power *exp.

```
double ldexp(double x, int exp);
```

Multiplies x by 2 raised to the exp power.

```
double log(double x);
```

Computes the natural logarithm of x.

```
double log10(double x);
```

Computes the base-10 logarithm of x.

```
double modf(double value, double *iptr);
```

Breaks the argument value into integral and fractional parts. It returns the fractional part, and stores the integral part at *iptr.

```
double pow(double x, double y);
```

Computes x raised to the power y.

```
double sin(double x);
```

Computes the sine of x.

```
double sinh(double x);
```

Computes the hyperbolic sine of x.

```
double sqrt(double x);
```

Computes the square root of x.

```
double tan(double x);
```

Computes the tangent of x.

```
double tanh(double x);
```

Computes the hyperbolic tangent of x.

[LOCAL NOTES]

NAME

6.11_setjmp - non-local jumps <setjmp.h>

The functions `setjmp` and `longjmp` provide a facility whereby one function, arbitrarily deep in the calling tree, can cause control to resume at a previously-encountered point higher in the calling tree. Here are the contents of the header:

`jmp_buf`

is a array type suitable for holding the "return-to-here" information.

`int setjmp(jmp_buf env);`

saves information about its calling environment in the `jmp_buf` array accessed through `env`. (By the usual C conversions, `env` is actually a pointer to the first element of the specified array.) If a `longjmp` is ever executed using this `jmp_buf` information, execution will suddenly resume at the return from the `setjmp` function. In other words, the flow of control "looks like" an ordinary return from `setjmp`. If the returned value from `setjmp` is zero, it is the ordinary direct return from calling `setjmp`. If the returned value is non-zero, it is the value being passed from an invocation of `longjmp` somewhere.

`void longjmp(jmp_buf env, int val);`

causes a return to the invocation of `setjmp` which established the `jmp_buf` information used in the call. The integer `val` is passed back as the returned value; if `val` was (inadvertently) equal to zero, it is changed to a `1`.

Only `volatile` and static values are guaranteed to be preserved across `setjmp`/`longjmp` calls. The ordinary (non-`volatile`) automatic variables of the function that called `setjmp` may be in an indeterminate state if they have changed between the calls to `setjmp` and `longjmp`.

In a strictly conforming (maximally portable) program, the `setjmp` function can only be called in these contexts:

```
switch (setjmp(env))    /* or ... */
if (setjmp(env) == 0)   /* or ... */
if (setjmp(env) != 0)
```

[LOCAL NOTES]

[LOCAL NOTES]

NAME

6.12_signal - signal handling `<signal.h>`

A "signal" is an interrupt, which can be generated either by hardware or by software. The Standard Library provides a signal-handling capability, essentially as originally defined in UNIX 7th Edition. The `<signal.h>` header defines one type:

sig_atomic_t

is the integral type of an object which can be modified as an "atomic" entity, even in the presence of asynchronous interrupts. In a byte-oriented machine, it would typically be char; in a word-oriented machine, it would typically be int.

There are several named constants. The first named constant is suitable for comparison against the returned value from the signal function:

SIG_ERR   signifies that the request could not be honored

Two named constants are suitable for passing as the second argument to the signal function; these two are used to make certain requests of the signal function.

SIG_DFL   establish system-default handling for this signal

SIG_IGN   ignore this signal

The other named constants are integer constants suitable for passing as the first argument to the signal function; they indicate which signal is being handled:

SIGABRT   abnormal termination

SIGFPE   zero divide, overflow, or other arithmetic error

SIGILL   illegal instruction

SIGINT   interactive attention signal (BREAK key, control-C, etc.)

SIGSEGV   segmentation error, invalid storage access

SIGTERM   termination request sent to the program

An implementation is not obliged to generate any or all of these signals with asynchronous interrupts. If no asynchronous interrupts are supported, the named constants are simply available for use in a raise call. Each implementation may provide other named constants, whose names begin with the letters SIG and an uppercase letter.

There are two functions declared in `<signal.h>`: `raise` and `signal`.

```
int raise(int sig);
```

> sends the specified signal to the executing program. What happens then is dependent upon any prior invocations of the `signal` function:

```
void (*signal(int sig, void (*func)(int)))(int);
```

> If the second argument to `signal` is `SIG_IGN`, the specified signal will henceforth be ignored. Thus,
>
> ```
> signal(SIGINT, SIG_IGN);
> ```
>
> causes the keyboard "attention interrupt" to be ignored. If the second argument is `SIG_DFL`, the specified signal will be handled in a default manner by the system. (Typically, but not universally, the default action for "attention interrupt" is to terminate program execution.) Otherwise, the second argument should be the address of a "signal-handler" function for the specified signal.

The simplest and most reliable handler simply sets a flag and returns. Here, for example, is how the keyboard "attention interrupt" can be handled:

```
volatile sig_atomic_t attn_flag = 0;
void attn_handler(int);
void subfn(void);
int main()
    {
    /* ... */
    signal(SIGINT, attn_handler);
    /* ... */
    subfn();
    exit(0);
    }
void subfn(void)
    {
    while (more_transactions)
        {
        if (attn_flag != 0)
            {
            attn_flag = 0;
            /* now respond to the interrupt, */
            /* possibly calling the longjmp function for restart */
            }
        /* ... */
        }
    }
void attn_handler(int sig)
    {
    attn_flag = 1;
    signal(SIGINT, attn_handler);   /* re-establish handler */
    }
```

None of the library functions (except for signal itself) are guaranteed to be re-entrant, so none of them can be used with portable reliability in a signal handler that executes a return.

Signal handlers that execute longjmp are especially unreliable in portable code, because interrupts can occur during the updating of in-memory FILE structures, data-base indexes, etc., which could be left in an incompletely-updated state.

On the other hand, in system-specific programs which use low-level operating-system calls (such as is common in UNIX programming), the invocation of the system call may be terminated prematurely by receipt of a signal. The alternatives are system-dependent and version-dependent.

[LOCAL NOTES]

[LOCAL NOTES]

NAME

   6.13_stdarg - variable-argument access `<stdarg.h>`

The `<stdarg.h>` header provides a portable method for accessing variable-length argument lists. A function that uses this method can access its named parameters directly, just by using their names as usual. But it can also access further, un-named argument values which were passed by the calling function.

The header `<stdarg.h>` provides one named type (`va_list`) and three macros (`va_start`, `va_arg`, `va_end`). The macros are described as if they were functions, but certain liberties are taken: the name *parmN* designates the name of the rightmost parameter in the parameter list of the function that invokes these macros, and *type* is an actual type, such as `int` or `double`. More precisely, it must be a type to which a trailing asterisk can be attached. Thus, to accept a pointer-to-function argument, use a `typedef`'ed name:

```
typedef void (*VOIDFN)(int);
/* ... */
pf = va_arg(ap, VOIDFN);
```

`va_list`

   is a named type for an "argument-walking" variable. In the examples below, the variable `ap` will have the type `va_list`.

`void va_start(va_list ap, ` *parmN*`);`

   Before accessing the un-named argument values, the `va_start` macro must be called, with the name of the `va_list` variable and the name of the right-most named parameter. This initializes the `va_list` variable.

type `va_arg(va_list ap, ` *type*`);`

   accesses the next un-named argument value, whose type is specified as the *type* parameter. The argument value will have been promoted according to the default argument promotions, widening small integers to `int` and `float`'s to `double`. Thus, the *type* parameter should specify the widened type. For example, it would always be an error to specify `char` as the *type* parameter.

`void va_end(va_list ap);`

   should be invoked after the last access to un-named arguments.

An example may help to clarify the behavior. Consider a function which accepts a varying number of string arguments and catenates them together into one destination string. No such function is in the Standard Library, but we could invent one (`stringer`, say) and invoke it like this:

```
stringer(buf, string1, string2, string3, NULL)
```

The definition of stringer would look like this:

```
#include <stdarg.h>
char *stringer(
    char *init_dest,        /* original pointer to destination */
    const char *s,          /* the first source string */
    ...)                    /* "ellipsis" -- more un-named args */
{
    va_list ap;                         /* the "argument-walker" */
    register char *dest = init_dest;    /* pointer to destination */
    register const char *src;           /* pointer to next source */

    va_start(ap, s);
    for (src = s; src != NULL; src = va_arg(ap, const char *))
        while (*src != '\0')
            *dest++ = *src++;
    *dest = '\0';
    va_end(ap);
    return init_dest;
}
```

In the for loop of stringer, the initialization (src = s) starts src with the first source string; this one has the name s. The re-initialization (or "step") of the for sets src to va_arg(ap, const char *), which produces the value of the next (un-named) argument, whose type is const char *. The loop terminates when src has received the null pointer value; this is how the function knows how many arguments were passed.

[LOCAL NOTES]

NAME
    6.14_stdio - input/output <stdio.h>

The header <stdio.h> declares all the functions that handle input and output, along with several types and macros.

When these brief descriptions say that "zero means success", it means that a returned value of zero indicates success; a non-zero return, indicating failure, is usually accompanied by the setting of errno to an implementation-defined error code.

Here are the types and macros:

BUFSIZ   size of the buffer used by setbuf

EOF   negative integral value that indicates end-of-file

FILE   type for controlling a file (see fopen)

FILENAME_MAX   size of array large enough for a long file name

FOPEN_MAX   minimum number of simultaneously open files

fpos_t   type for specifying file position (see fgetpos)

_IOFBF   constant for "full buffering" (see setvbuf)

_IOLBF   constant for "line buffering" (see setvbuf)

_IONBF   constant for "no buffering" (see setvbuf)

L_tmpnam   size of array large enough for temporary file name

NULL   a null pointer constant

SEEK_CUR   constant for "relative to current position"

SEEK_END   constant for "relative to end of file"

SEEK_SET   constant for "relative to start of file" (see fseek)

stderr   pointer to the standard error FILE

stdin   pointer to the standard input FILE

stdout   pointer to the standard output FILE

TMP_MAX   minimum number of unique names from tmpnam

These are the functions in the <stdio.h> header of Standard C:

Copyright © Plum Hall Inc 1989

```
void clearerr(FILE *stream);
```

clears the end-of-file and error indicators of stream.

```
int fclose(FILE *stream);
```

flushes the stream and closes the file. Zero means success.

```
void feof(FILE *stream);
```

tests the end-of-file indicator of stream.

```
void ferror(FILE *stream);
```

tests the error indicator of stream.

```
int fflush(FILE *stream);
```

flushes the output buffer (for an output or update stream), or undoes the effect of any preceding ungetc (for an input stream). Zero means success. Calling fflush(NULL) flushes all output streams.

```
int fgetc(FILE *stream);
```

reads one character from stream.

```
int fgetpos(FILE *stream, fpos_t *pos);
```

stores the current file position in *pos. Zero means success. (The functions fgetpos and fsetpos are required because the long integers used by fseek are too small to record file positions on various large, record-oriented systems.)

```
char *fgets(char *s, int n, FILE *stream);
```

reads into s at most n-1 characters from stream, and appends a null-terminator character. It returns NULL on end-of-file or error; otherwise it returns s.

```
FILE *fopen(const char *name, const char *mode);
```

opens the file by name, according to mode.

Each of the familiar "r", "w", "a" mode's can have a trailing plus-sign modifier that specifies a new mode:

r+   open for update (reading and writing)

w+   create for update, or truncate to zero length

a+   append; open or create for update, writing at end-of-file

There is one further augmentation: UNIX systems are unique in making no distinction between a "text" file and a "binary" file. To provide a more portable library, the committee allowed the letter b at the end of the mode argument to fopen (or just preceding a + modifier). Thus,

```
        fp = fopen("pmt.dat", "rb");
```

opens a binary file named pmt.dat for reading. The absence of the
b indicates a "text" file.

```
int fprintf(FILE *stream, const char *format, ...);
```

writes to stream according to the format and various arguments that
may follow. It returns the number of characters transmitted, or a
negative number if an output error occurred.

The Standard C versions of the printf functions have considerably
more features than the original Kernighan & Ritchie version. The
following table will illustrate more clearly the differences. The
notation k means K&R, and s means Standard C.

```
        Comparison of  printf  capabilities


        Start:  %       K   S   start conversion specifier

        Flags:  -       K   S   left-adjust
                +           S   print '+' or '-' sign
                space       S   print ' ' or '-' sign
                #           S   "alternate" forms

        Width:  0       K   S   leading zeroes
                number  K   S   minimum output field width
                *           S   take width from next arg

        Precis: *           S   take precision from next arg
                number  K   S   floating precision or max string width
```

```
Conv:   d    K  S   decimal int
        o    K  S   octal unsigned int
        x    K  S   hexadecimal unsigned int
        u    K  S   decimal unsigned int
        l    K  S   (with int conv) long
        f    K  S   "[-]ddd.ddd" fixed-point
        e    K  S   "[-]d.ddde+dd"
        g    K  S   smaller of 'e' and 'f'
        c    K  S   character
        s    K  S   string
        X       S   hexadecimal with caps "ABCDEF"
        i       S   decimal int
        h       S   (with int conv) short
        E       S   "[-]d.dddE+dd"
        G       S   smaller of 'E' and 'f'
        L       S   (with floating conv) long double
        p       S   value of pointer
        n       S   store number of chars printed so far
```

`int fputc(int c, FILE *stream);`

> writes one character to stream.

`int fputs(const char *s, FILE *stream);`

> writes the string s out onto stream. It returns EOF on error, otherwise a non-negative value.

`size_t fread(void *ptr, size_t size, size_t nmemb, FILE *stream);`

> reads, into the storage specified by ptr, up to nmemb objects of size size, from stream. The number of objects successfully read is returned.

`FILE *freopen(const char *fname, const char *mode, FILE *stream);`

> opens the file specified by fname, and associates it with stream. The mode argument is used as in the fopen function.

`int fscanf(FILE *stream, const char *format, ...);`

> reads input from stream according to the format and successive pointer arguments. It returns EOF if end-of-file occurs before any input conversion; otherwise, it returns the number of input assignments.

> As with the printf functions, the scanf functions have gained many new capabilities:

Comparison of scanf capabilities

Whitespace:	K		ignored(!)
		S	matches whitespace input
Start: %	K	S	start conversion specifier
Flags: *	K	S	suppresses assignment
Width: number	K	S	maximum input field width
Conv: d	K	S	decimal int
o	K	S	octal unsigned int
x	K	S	hexadecimal unsigned int
l	K	S	(with int conv) long
f	K	S	float
e	K	S	float
l	K	S	(with floating conv) double
c	K	S	character
s	K	S	string (one "word")
h	K		(by itself) decimal short int
h		S	(with int conv) short
u		S	decimal unsigned int
X		S	hexadecimal unsigned int
i		S	int: 0x->hex, 0->octal, else decimal
E		S	float
g		S	float
G		S	float
L		S	(with floating conv) long double
[list]		S	string of chars from "list"
[^list]		S	string of chars not in "list"
p		S	value of pointer
n		S	store number of chars read so far

```
int fseek(FILE *stream, long offset, int whence);
```

sets the file position indicator, and clears the end-of-file indicator, for the specified stream. The possible values of whence are named by SEEK_SET, SEEK_CUR, and SEEK_END (as described above). Zero means success.

```
int fsetpos(FILE *stream, const fpos_t *pos);
```

sets the file position indicator for the specified stream. Zero means success.

```
long ftell(FILE *stream);
```

reports the current value of the file position indicator. On failure, ftell returns -1L and sets errno.

```
size_t fwrite(const void *ptr, size_t size, size_t nmemb, FILE *stream);
```

> writes, from the storage specified by ptr, up to nmemb objects of size size, to stream. The number of objects successfully written is returned.

```
int getc(FILE *stream);
```

> is equivalent to fgetc, except that it may be an "unprotected" macro.

```
getchar(void);
```

> is equivalent to getc(stdin).

```
char *gets(char *s);
```

> reads characters from the standard input into the string s until a newline is read or end-of-file is reached. Any newline is discarded. A null-pointer return indicates either end-of-file or a read error.

```
void perror(const char *s);
```

> prints, on the standard error file, an error message that reflects the current value of errno and incorporates the string s (if non-null).

```
int printf(const char *format, ...);
```

> is equivalent to an fprintf call that uses stdout. (See fprintf.)

```
int putc(int c, FILE *stream);
```

> is equivalent to fputc, except that it may be an "unprotected" macro.

```
int putchar(int c);
```

> is equivalent to putc(c, stdout).

```
int puts(const char *s);
```

> writes the string s, followed by a newline, to the standard output. Zero means success.

```
int remove(const char *filename);
```

> causes the specified file to be removed. If the file is open, the behavior is implementation-defined. Zero means success.

```
int rename(const char *old, const char *new);
```

> changes the name of the file old to new. If a file named new already exists, the behavior is implementation-defined. Zero means success.

```
void rewind(FILE *stream);
```

sets the file position indicator for stream to the beginning of the file, and clears stream's error indicator.

```
int scanf(const char *format, ...);
```

is equivalent to an fscanf call that uses stdin.

```
void setbuf(FILE *stream, char *buf);
```

requests "no buffering" if buf is null; otherwise it requests "full buffering" using buf for buffer space.

```
int setvbuf(FILE *stream, char *buf, int mode, size_t size);
```

can be called after opening but before using stream. According to the value of mode, it requests full buffering (_IOFBF), line buffering (_IOLBF), or no buffering (_IONBF). Specifying a non-null buf (whose size is size) requests that buf be used instead of an automatically-allocated buffer. Zero means success.

```
FILE *tmpfile(void);
```

creates a temporary binary file (opened for update) that will automatically be removed when it is closed or when the program terminates. A null-pointer return indicates failure.

```
int sprintf(char *s, const char *format, ...);
```

is equivalent to fprintf, except that characters are written into the string s rather than to a file. A null-terminator character is appended to s.

```
int sscanf(const char *s, const char *format, ...);
```

is equivalent to fscanf, except that input is taken from the string s, rather than from a file.

```
char *tmpnam(char *s);
```

generates a file-name string that should be unique. If s is non-null, the name is generated into s and that address is returned. If s is null, the name is generated into a static location, and that address is returned.

```
int ungetc(int c, FILE *stream);
```

"pushes back" c (after conversion to unsigned char) onto stream; in other words, the next character read from that stream will be c. An intervening call to fflush, fseek, fsetpos, or rewind discards any pushed-back characters. The pushed-back character is returned, or EOF if failure.

```
int vfprintf(FILE *stream, const char *format, va_list arg);
```

is equivalent to fprintf, with the variable-length argument list replaced by a va_list argument (which should already have been initialized by va_start prior to calling vfprintf). This function (and the two functions that follow) requires <stdarg.h> as well as <stdio.h>.

```
int vprintf(const char *format, va_list arg);
```

is equivalent to printf, with the variable-length argument list replaced by a va_list argument.

```
int vsprintf(char *s, const char *format, va_list arg);
```

is equivalent to sprintf, with the variable-length argument list replaced by a va_list argument.

The remainder of this section will describe a miscellaneous set of revisions and clarifications regarding input-output functions.

None of the functions involving "file descriptors" (open, close, read, write, lseek, fdopen) are in the Standard Library. Arguments for this decision: there are technical problems in creating a uniform specification for all systems; these are not the most efficient primitives on some systems; the relationship with the "stream" I/O functions is very tightly coupled under UNIX systems; if fread, fwrite, fseek, fgets, and fputs are efficiently implemented (especially for "unbuffered" modes), they can equal the low-level performance; specifying two overlapping sets of functions is difficult and wasteful of effort; and each system which currently supports them has slightly different options and behaviors. Arguments in favor of standardizing them: they are part of the "C culture"; lots of code uses them; standards are needed because of all the "slightly different" systems. The arguments against standardizing them prevailed.

A line in a text file can contain zero characters (plus newline). This is a clarification, not a change. Trailing spaces may be stripped from text file lines, in some systems.

Opening, then closing, an output stream may leave a non-existent file, rather than an empty file, in some systems.

The fflush function (as well as fseek and rewind) allows a transition from reading to writing or vice-versa.

After a function call such as

```
rename("oldfile", "newfile")
```

if the file newfile already exists, the result is implementation-defined. Some systems delete the old file, some refuse to rename, some create a new "version" of newfile. For maximum portability, execute

```
remove("newfile");
```

before doing the rename, if the prior existence of newfile is truly immaterial.

The scanf functions can push back at most one character of input. They never produce a null string result. Thus the format %[^:] ("any characters except colon") gives a "matching error" if the very next input character is a colon; this terminates the scan.

The ungetc function will, in general, back up the file position indicator, if the file is "binary". If the file is "text", the backup behavior is unspecified; i.e., some systems do it and some don't. (On some non-UNIX systems, relative file positioning is very expensive for text files.) It is still permissible to ungetc at the beginning of the file, but the resulting file position indicator is undefined.

Each call to fseek clears the associated end-of-file indicator. Most libraries already work this way, but the documentation often disagrees.

The function perror prints a message, just as in UNIX systems. A new function strerror provides an in-memory message string. (See 6.16_string.)

[LOCAL NOTES]

[LOCAL NOTES]

NAME
     6.15_stdlib - general utilities <stdlib.h>

The header <stdlib.h> is the "miscellaneous bin" into which the otherwise-uncategorized functions are grouped. It declares two types and several named constants:

div_t   a structure type for the returned value from div

ldiv_t   a structure type for the returned value from ldiv

RAND_MAX   the maximum value returned by rand

MB_CUR_MAX   maximum size of multibyte character in this locale

EXIT_SUCCESS   exit status for successful termination

EXIT_FAILURE   exit status for failure termination

These are the functions in the general utilities library:

void abort(void);

> causes an abnormal program termination, by calling raise(SIGABRT); in case control returns after the raise call, abort then calls exit with an unsuccessful termination status. Any actions such as flushing buffers or closing files are implementation-defined.

int abs(int j);

> returns the absolute value of j.

int atexit(void (*func)(void));

> puts the function pointed to by func onto a list of functions ("exit handlers") that will be invoked at normal program termination. At least 32 exit handlers may be so registered. Zero means success.

double atof(const char *nptr);

> produces a double result by conversion from the string nptr.

int atoi(const char *nptr);

> produces a int result by conversion from the string nptr.

long atol(const char *nptr);

> produces a long result by conversion from the string nptr.

```
void *bsearch(
    const void *key,
    const void *base,
    size_t nmemb,
    size_t size,
    int (*compar)(const void *, const void *));
```

> searches a sorted array of nmemb objects, located at base, each of which is of size size, for a member which matches the object pointed to by key. The comparison logic to be used is specified by the *compar function. If no match is found, a null pointer is returned; otherwise, a pointer to the matching object is returned.

```
void *calloc(size_t nmemb, size_t size);
```

> allocates space (in the "heap") for an array of nmemb objects, each of whose size is size. The space is initialized to bitwise zeros. If nmemb*size is zero, the behavior is implementation-defined.

```
div_t div(int numer, int denom);
```

> computes the quotient and remainder of numer/denom. The div_t type is a structure containing int members named quot and rem. The quotient is truncated toward zero, and the remainder (if non-zero) has the same sign as the quotient. (Note that this function could provide in-line code, as described early in this section, but it can not be used for a mathematical "modulus" function, because the remainder can be negative.)

```
void exit(int status);
```

> causes a "normal program termination". Because of the difficulties of handling return codes on various operating systems, the behavior of the exit function is somewhat implementation-defined. Calling exit(0) causes a *success* code to be returned, as always. However, all other exit arguments have implementation-defined semantics. In particular, exit(1) has always, and may in the future, indicate *success* on some (non-UNIX) systems. The status codes EXIT_SUCCESS and EXIT_FAILURE may be used for portability.

```
void free(void *ptr);
```

> causes the pointed-to space to be made available for further allocation. If ptr is a null pointer, no action occurs.

183

```
char *getenv(const char *name);
```

searches the implementation's "environment" for a string that matches the name string, and returns a pointer to that string. If no match, a null pointer is returned. A strictly portable program should not modify the storage accessed by getenv. Furthermore, the pointer returned by getenv might point to a static area that would be over-written on subsequent calls to getenv. Thus, it may be necessary to copy the accessed string:

```
        strfit(mystorage, getenv("NAME"), N);
```

```
long labs(long j);
```

returns the absolute value of j.

```
ldiv_t ldiv(long numer, long denom);
```

produces a quotient and remainder, similarly to the div function above.

```
void *malloc(size_t size);
```

allocates space for an object of size bytes, and returns a pointer to it. If size is zero, the behavior is implementation-defined.

```
int mblen(const char *s, size_t n);
```

tells the number of bytes in the multibyte character (of at most n bytes) at *s.

```
size_t mbstowcs(wchar_t *pwcs, const char *s, size_t n);
```

converts from the multibyte string at *s into at most n wide characters at *pwcs.

```
int mbtowc(wchar_t *pwc, const char *s, size_t n);
```

converts the multibyte character at *s into a single wchar_t integer at *pwc.

```
void qsort(
    void *base,
    size_t nmemb,
    size_t size,
    int (*compar)(const void *, const void *));
```

sorts an array of nmemb objects, each of size bytes, located at base. The ordering logic is provided by the function pointed to by compar. This function will be called inside qsort with addresses of the objects to be compared.

`int rand(void);`

> returns a pseudo-random number in the range 0 to RAND_MAX. (The minimum value for RAND_MAX is 32767.)

`void *realloc(void *ptr, size_t size);`

> allocates space for an object of `size` bytes. The `ptr` argument should point to previously-allocated space; the contents of the new object will be unchanged, up to the lesser of the old and new sizes. (If `size` is zero, the behavior is implementation-defined.)

`void srand(unsigned seed);`

> sets the seed of the pseudo-random generation sequence.

`double strtod(const char *nptr, char **endptr);`

> produces a `double` result by conversion from the string `nptr`. If the argument `endptr` is non-null, the `char *` pointer at `*endptr` is assigned the address of the first ("unrecognized") character past the converted portion of the string. In other words, `*endptr` can be used to tell where the conversion "left off". Also, if `endptr` is not null, and the string is empty or invalid, `*endptr` is assigned the value `nptr`, providing a quick test for "invalid input". The "str-to" functions (`strtod`, `strtol`, `strtoul`) all check properly for overflows and underflows, and set their returned values and `errno` accordingly.

`long strtol(const char *nptr, char **endptr, int base);`

> produces a `long` result by conversion from the string `nptr`, using `base` as the number base. The letters `a` (or `A`) through `z` (or `Z`) are ascribed the values 10 to 35. If `base` is 16, a leading `0x` (or `0X`) is permitted in the string. If `base` is zero, the string is interpreted according to C-language constant rules for decimal, octal, or hexadecimal forms in the string. The `endptr` argument is used as in `strtod` above.

`unsigned long strtoul(const char *nptr, char **endptr, int base);`

> behaves just like `strtol`, to produce an `unsigned long` result.

`int system(const char *string);`

> passes `string` (if non-null) to the host environment for (environment-dependent) interpretation by a "command processor". If `string` is a null pointer, `system` returns zero if and only if the environment has a command processor. Otherwise, the returned value is implementation-defined. (If possible, the function should return the "return code" produced by the executed command.)


```
int wctomb(char *s, wchar_t wchar);
```

converts the wide character wchar into a multibyte string at *s.

```
size_t wcstombs(char *s, const wchar_t *pwcs, size_t n);
```

converts a sequence of wide characters at *pwcs into a multibyte string at *ps.

[LOCAL NOTES]

[LOCAL NOTES]

NAME

    6.16_string - string handling `<string.h>`

This header collects several useful functions for manipulating strings and byte arrays. Only four of them are familiar from K&R (`strcat`, `strcmp`, `strcpy`, `strlen`) but most of the others have appeared in more recent C libraries. In all of these functions, if copying takes place beyond the end of the target object, the behavior is undefined. In all but `memmove`, if source and target objects overlap, the behavior is undefined.

`void *memchr(const void *s, int c, size_t n);`

    produces a pointer to the first occurrence of `c` (converted to `unsigned char`) in `s`. It returns a null pointer if there is no match.

`int memcmp(const void *s1, const void *s2, size_t n);`

    returns a negative, zero, or positive integer according to the comparison of the `n` bytes of `s1` and `s2`.

`void *memcpy(void *s1, const void *s2, size_t n);`

    copies `n` bytes from `s2` into `s1`. If those `n`-byte objects overlap, the behavior is undefined.

`void *memmove(void *s1, const void *s2, size_t n);`

    behaves just like `memcpy`, except that overlapping moves work properly. In other words, `memcpy` is the "fast" function, and `memmove` is the "safe" function.

`void *memset(void *s, int c, size_t n);`

    fills `n` bytes of `s` with `c` (converted to `unsigned char`), and returns `s`.

`char *strcat(char *s1, const char *s2);`

    catenates the characters of the string `s2` onto the end of the string `s1`.

`char *strchr(const char *s, int c);`

    returns a pointer to the first occurrence of `c` (converted to `char`) in the string `s`, or a null pointer if there is no match.

`int strcmp(const char *s1, const char *s2);`

    returns a negative, zero, or positive integer according to the comparison of the bytes of `s1` and `s2`.

`int strcoll(const char *s1, const char *s2);`

behaves just like `strcmp`, except that it applies the locale-specific collating rules determined by the `setlocale` function. (See `setlocale` in 6.9_locale above.)

`char *strcpy(char *s1, const char *s2);`

copies the string `s2` into the storage specified by `s1`. Overlapping moves give an undefined result.

`size_t strcspn(const char *s1, const char *s2);`

computes the length of the initial segment of `s1` which consists of characters *not* in the string `s2`.

`char *strerror(int errnum);`

maps the error number `errnum` into an (implementation-defined) error message string. Since the string could be in a static table, or in a re-useable buffer, it may be necessary to copy the string:

```
strfit(mybuffer, strerror(errnum), N);
```

`size_t strlen(const char *s);`

returns the length of the string `s`.

`char *strncat(char *s1, const char *s2, size_t n);`

appends not more than `n` characters of `s2` onto `s1`, and null-terminates the result.

`int strncmp(const char *s1, const char *s2, size_t n);`

returns a negative, zero, or positive integer according to the comparison of at most `n` characters of `s1` and `s2`.

`char *strncpy(char *s1, const char *s2, size_t n);`

copies at most `n` characters from `s2` into `s1`. Overlapping moves give undefined behavior. If the length of `s2` is smaller than `n`, null-character padding will be added; otherwise, the result will not be null-terminated.

`char *strpbrk(const char *s1, const char *s2);`

returns a pointer to the first occurrence in `s1` of any character in `s2`.

`char *strrchr(const char *s, int c);`

returns a pointer to the last occurrence in `s` of `c` (converted to `char`), or a null pointer if there is no match.

189

`size_t strspn(const char *s1, const char *s2);`

> returns the length of the initial segment of s1 which consists entirely of characters from s2.

`char *strstr(const char *s1, const char *s2);`

> locates the first occurrence in s1 of the sequence of characters in s2, or a null pointer if there is no match.

`char *strtok(char *s1, char *s2);`

> is used to break the string s1 into a series of "tokens" delimited by characters in s2. (The function has not changed; it is as complicated as ever. See the Standard, or a manual, or *RDS* for details.)

`size_t strxfrm(char *to, const char *from, size_t maxsize);`

> transforms from into a locale-specific "sorting key" in to, whose size is maxsize. (See setlocale, in 6.9_locale above.)

[LOCAL NOTES]

[LOCAL NOTES]

NAME

6.17_time - date and time `<time.h>`

Various functions for dealing with dates and times are provided in `<time.h>`. These are the named types and named constants:

`clock_t`   an arithmetic type for representing CPU times

`time_t`   an arithmetic type for representing date-and-time

`struct tm`   a structure type for "broken-down time":

```
struct tm {
        int tm_sec;      /* seconds {0:60} (allow for leap-second) */
        int tm_min;      /* minutes {0:59} */
        int tm_hour;     /* hours {0:23} */
        int tm_mday;     /* day of the month {1:31} */
        int tm_mon;      /* month of the year {0:11} */
        int tm_year;     /* years since 1900 A.D. */
        int tm_wday;     /* days since previous Sunday {0:6} */
        int tm_yday;     /* day of the year {0:365} */
        int tm_isdst;    /* positive for daylight savings time */
        /* ... other orderings and other members are allowed ... */
        };
```

`CLOCKS_PER_SEC` number of `clock_t` units per second

`char *asctime(const struct tm *timeptr);`

converts the `struct tm` "broken-down time" into a string in this form:

```
Sun Sep 16 01:03:52 1973\n\0
```

`clock_t clock(void);`

produces a `clock_t` representation of CPU time since some implementation-defined starting point. It returns `(clock_t)-1` if CPU time is unavailable.

`char *ctime(time_t *timer);`

converts the `time_t` time at `*timer` to a string of the form shown in `asctime` above.

`double difftime(time_t time1, time_t time0);`

Copyright © Plum Hall Inc 1989

produces (in seconds) the elapsed time from time0 to time1.

`struct tm *gmtime(const time_t *timeptr);`

converts the `time_t` at `*timeptr` to a "broken-down time", expressed as Coordinated Universal Time (UTC), or a null pointer if UTC is not available. (The function name derived from earlier use of Greenwich Mean Time, GMT.)

`struct tm *localtime(const time_t *timer);`

converts the `time_t` at `*timer` to a "broken-down time", expressed as local time.

`time_t mktime(struct tm *timeptr);`

converts the "broken-down time" at `*timeptr` into `time_t` time, or into `(time_t)-1` if the result is unrepresentable. It also "normalizes" the components of `*timeptr`, bringing all of them into their specified ranges.

`size_t strftime(char *s, size_t size, const char *fmt, const struct tm *timeptr);`

converts the "broken-down time" at `*timeptr` into the string `s` (whose size is `size`) in a locale-specific way according to time formats in `fmt`. (See `setlocale`, above.)

`time_t time(time_t *timer);`

returns the current date-and-time as a `time_t`. If `timer` is non-null, it also stores the date-and-time in `*timer`.

[LOCAL NOTES]

NAME

   7.1_review - first-order correctness review and test

The programming field could use a "generally accepted" criterion for a reasonable amount of review and testing. It is time to bring some over-simplification to an overly-complicated problem.

What we need is a procedure which could be taught in one session of any programming course, to serve as a reasonable minimum upon program verification. Too often, we now teach programming like a driver-instruction course that omits mention of brakes.

Each particular development standard requires different deliverables, but they all include source code (at least). The proposal described here is that the source code should be accompanied by a specific set of review notes. If testing is part of the programmer's job, a specific criterion for testing should also be followed.

The procedures are called *first-order correctness review* and *first-order correctness test*.

WHAT IS A FIRST-ORDER CORRECTNESS REVIEW AND TEST

In *Learning to Program in C* are described two criteria (adapted from Glen Myers' *Art of Software Testing*):

Boundary values (limits upon program performance): Each valid boundary value should be tested, and the adjacent invalid value should also be tested.

Distinct cases (or "equivalence classes"): Each distinct behavior of the program should be exercised by one representative test case.

From the original specification, different input cases, different output cases, and different internal states all suggest distinct cases to be tested. From the program source listing, further distinct cases can be systematically listed by considering what data values are required to make each individual conditional to be *TRUE* in one case and *FALSE* in some other case. (This means that tests for "all distinct cases" are a superset of the tests for "branch coverage", which forces every potential branch to be executed.)

A *first-order test*, then, is one which meets these criteria.

A *first-order review* is one which produces an on-paper list of the cases which would be needed for a first-order test. The agenda for the code review is the actual production of this list.

Besides testable cases, the review should identify "untestable" exception cases. In a reliable program, each exception case is prevented from happening by some guarantee elsewhere in the program, or in the documentation, the specification, or the language standard. The review should document each such guarantee.

The exception cases can be indicated by abbreviations such as this:

ABBREV	OPERATORS			DESCRIPTION OF EXCEPTION CASES
OOB	a[n]	a<<n	a>>n	"Out Of Bounds" subscript or shift count
BAD_P	*p	p[n]	p->m	"Bad pointer" -- out-of-bounds, dangling, or null pointer
OFLO	a*b ++a --a	a+b a++ a--	a-b	"Overflow" -- a signed-arithmetic or pointer expression overflow
UFLO	a*b a+b	a/b a-b		"Underflow" -- a floating-point expression result too small to represent
CHOP	a=b	f(a)		"Chop" or "Truncation" -- assignment, or calling prototyped-function, that loses bits
DIV_0	a/b	a%b		"Divide-by-zero"
XALIGN	(ptr *)			"Mis-alignment" -- a pointer cast that loses alignment information

A similar table should be produced for each library of called functions used by the application, and used in the review of exceptions and distinct cases. (The simple example below calls no library functions.)

These review and test procedures are called "first-order" because there is no attempt to deal with the (combinatorially-large) set of interactions between individual conditionals; each one is analyzed independently.

HOW TO DO A FIRST-ORDER REVIEW

Let us examine a specific little example, and show what a first-order review would produce. Consider a portable C implementation of the Standard Library function strcmp, which is now required to use unsigned char logic in comparisons:

```
1   /* strcmp - compare (unsigned) strings  */
2   int strcmp(
3       register const char s[],   /* : string */
4       register const char t[])   /* : string */
5       {
6       typedef unsigned char uchar;
7
8       while (*s != '\0' && *s == *t)
9           {
10          ++s;
11          ++t;
12          }
13      if (*(uchar *)s < *(uchar *)t)
14          return -1;
15      else if (*(uchar *)s == *(uchar *)t)
16          return 0;
17      else
18          return 1;
19      }
```

The review proceeds through the program line-by-line, identifying distinct cases, boundary values, and assumptions on each line.

On line 8, the logical-and condition has three possible outcomes: *FALSE* immediately, *TRUE* on the left and *FALSE* on the right, and both sides *TRUE*. The only possible exception is *BAD_P* ("bad pointer").

On lines 10 and 11, an *OFLO* is possible ("pointer wrap-around").

Line 13 has two testable outcomes (*FALSE* and *TRUE*). The pointer cast has a potential *XALIGN*.

On line 14 (the outcome when string s compares low to string t), the minimum boundary value for *s (considered as an unsigned char) is zero; the maximum boundary value for *t is UCHAR_MAX. There are no invalid values to test.

Line 15 has two Boolean outcomes, and no new exceptions.

Line 18 would be reached by a boundary case that matches the maximum *s with the minimum *t.

So far, the review notes look like this:


```
LIST OF TEST CASES    PROGRAM LISTING                          EXCEPTIONS?
-------------------   --------------------------------------   -----------
___F  ___TF  ___TT    8    while (*s != '\0' && *s == *t)      ___BAD_P
                      9    {
                      10        ++s;                           ___OFLO
                      11        ++t;                           ___OFLO
                      12   }
___F      ___T        13   if (*(uchar *)s < *(uchar *)t)      ___XALIGN
___MIN *s  ___MAX *t  14       return -1;
___F      ___T        15   else if (*(uchar *)s == *(uchar *)t)
                      16       return 0;
                      17   else
___MAX *s  ___MIN *t  18       return 1;
```

Next, the review returns to the specification. There are three distinct cases — low, equal, high — and these are assigned test cases numbered 1, 2, and 3.

The specification indicates that s and t must point to strings (i.e., properly null-terminated). This requirement will receive an item number soon.

The review notes look like this:

```
REVIEWER'S NOTES    SPECIFICATION
---------------     -----------------------------------------------
                    Outcomes of returned value:
___1___               Less than zero:    s compares low to t
___2___               Zero:              s compares equal to t
___3___               Greater than zero: s compares high to t
                    Parameters  s  and  t  must point to strings,
___                   properly null-terminated.
```

Now specific test cases are chosen, attempting wherever possible to use one case to cover both a boundary-value test and a distinct-case test:

```
TEST CASES AND DESCRIPTIONS
----------------------------------------------------------------

1.  s is null string, t starts with largest unsigned char value
2.  s and t are equal strings, e.g. "a"
3.  s starts with largest unsigned char value, t is null string
```

The review fills in the blanks next to each boundary-value and distinct-case test. In this example, the three cases chosen from the specification are sufficient to achieve both coverages.

Next, the review documents the reasons why each possible exception cannot happen:

197

GUARANTEES AGAINST EXCEPTIONS
----
4. Specification: strings s and t are null-terminated,
    so the pointer increments cannot overflow.
5. C Standard: unsigned char has the same alignment as char.

The annotated program listing now looks like this:

```
LIST OF TEST CASES     PROGRAM LISTING                              EXCEPTIONS?
------------------     --------------------------------------       ------------
 _1_F   _3_TF  _2_TT   8    while (*s != '\0' && *s == *t)           _4_BAD_P
                       9       {
                      10       ++s;                                  _4_OFLO
                      11       ++t;                                  _4_OFLO
                      12       }
 _3_F        _1_T     13    if (*(uchar *)s < *(uchar *)t)           _5_XALIGN
 _1_MIN *s  _1_MAX *t 14       return -1;
 _3_F        _2_T     15    else if (*(uchar *)s == *(uchar *)t)
                      16       return 0;
                      17    else
 _3_MAX *s  _3_MIN *t 18       return 1;
```

In this simple example, the actual program to apply the first-order test coverage is simple to construct:

```
TEST PROGRAM
------------------------------------------------------------------
#include <limits.h>
#include <assert.h>
#undef NDEBUG    /* turn on assert's */
char s_max[2] = {UCHAR_MAX, '\0'};   /* string with largest uchar */
int main()
    {
    assert(strcmp("", s_max) < 0);   /* case 1 */
    assert(strcmp("a", "a") == 0);   /* case 2 */
    assert(strcmp(s_max, "") > 0);   /* case 3 */
    exit(0);
    }
```

If an automated test-coverage analyzer is available ("branch-coverage" verifier), execution of this test driver can be shown mechanically to have covered all Boolean outcomes. Even more useful would be automated assistance in static checking of the exception-preventing guarantees ("Super-lint").

WHY THIS PARTICULAR APPROACH?

This methodology is suggested for projects and situations in which correctness and reliability are of paramount importance. (As an industry we may still undervalue these qualities in practice, but we all learn from experience.)

Mathematical techniques ("correctness proofs") have been suggested for this purpose, but most application areas are not formally axiomatized. Proofs, and other commendable approaches to analysis and design, do not by themselves supply a means of verifying that the design was properly implemented. Furthermore, many embedded applications interact with hardware and interfaces whose correct behavior cannot be formally assumed. Review, and subsequent testing, close the loop of verifiability.

Some people tout high-level languages that perform run-time checking as the path to reliability in practice. But a better approach is to *prevent* run-time exceptions by properly-coded program logic, not by patching up after they have occurred.

With regard to the review agenda, discussing the program in terms of specific test cases provides a language which is understandable to all parties — users, analysts, designers, and programmers. The first-order review discusses the program using systematically chosen examples.

As a practical matter, most of the first-order reviews that we have seen in practice have produced useful results — finding errors, improving documentation, or locating ambiguities in specifications. Plum Hall would be glad to hear about the experiences that your project has with techniques like this.

[This material first appeared as an article in **C Users Journal**, *December/January 1989, Vol 7, No 1, Pages 75-78.]*

NAME
    7.2_biblio - bibliography

ANSI X3J11. [1989]
    Draft Proposed American National Standard for Information Sys-
    tems — Programming Language C. X3 Secretariat: Computer and
    Business Equipment Manufacturers Association, 311 First St NW,
    Suite 500, Washington DC 20001, USA. (202-737-8888)

cummings, e. e. [1959]
    100 selected poems. Grove Press.

Gelperin, David, and Bill Hetzel. [1988]
    "The Growth of Software Testing". *Communications of the ACM*,
    Vol 31, No 6, Pp 687-695, June 1988.

IEEE 1003.1 [1989].
    Portable Operating System Interface for Computer Environments.
    (P1003.1 Draft). IEEE Computer Society, Technical Committee on
    Operating Systems, 345 East 47th Street, New York NY 10017,
    USA.

Jackson, M. A. [1975]
    Principles of Program Design. Academic Press.

Kernighan, Brian W., and Dennis M. Ritchie. [1978]
    The C Programming Language. Prentice-Hall.

Kernighan, Brian W., and P. J. Plauger. [1978]
    The Elements of Programming Style. McGraw-Hill.

Lister, Tim, and Tom DeMarco. [1987]
    Peopleware. Dorset House.

Myers, Glenford. [1979]
    The Art of Software Testing. John Wiley & Sons.

Myers, Glenford J. [1978]
    Composite/Structured Design. Van Nostrand Reinhold.

Plauger, P. J. [1988]
    Programming on Purpose. A series of articles in *Computer
    Language,* 1986-1988.

Plauger, P. J., and Jim Brodie [1989]
Standard C. Microsoft Press.

Plum, Thomas. [1983]
Learning to Program in C. Plum Hall.

Plum, Thomas. [1985]
Reliable Data Structures in C. Plum Hall.

Plum, Thomas, and Jim Brodie. [1985]
Efficient C. Plum Hall.

Plum, Thomas. [1989]
Learning to Program in C (Second Edition). Plum Hall.

Rochkind, Marc J. [1985]
Advanced UNIX Programming. Prentice-Hall.

Shore, John. [1988]
"Why I Never Met a Programmer I Could Trust". *Communications of the ACM.* Vol 31, No 4, Pp 372-375, April 1988.

Warnier, Jean Dominique. [1974]
Logical Construction of Programs. Van Nostrand Reinhold.

Wirth, Nicklaus. [1973]
Systematic Programming. Academic Press.

Yourdon, Edward, and Larry L. Constantine. [1979]
Structured Design. Prentice-Hall.

[LOCAL NOTES]

INDEX

In this index, items are identified by both page number and section number. For example, the citation "139(6.3)" refers to page 139, in section 6.3.

NAME

    reader_reply - Reader Reply Form

Please describe anything which would make *C Programming Guidelines* a better book for your purposes. (This includes, of course, typographical errors, bugs, and portability problems, but also any topics that received too much or too little emphasis.) We would also appreciate hearing what you liked best about the book.

NAME _____

COMPANY _____

ADDRESS _____

_____

CITY _____ STATE ____ ZIP _____

COUNTRY _____ PHONE _____

1

Plum Hall Inc
1 Spruce Ave
Cardiff, NJ 08232 USA

NAME

reader_reply - Reader Reply Form

Please describe anything which would make *C Programming Guidelines* a better book for your purposes. (This includes, of course, typographical errors, bugs, and portability problems, but also any topics that received too much or too little emphasis.) We would also appreciate hearing what you liked best about the book.

NAME _____

COMPANY _____

ADDRESS _____

_____

CITY _____ STATE _____ ZIP _____

COUNTRY _____ PHONE _____

1

Plum Hall Inc
1 Spruce Ave
Cardiff, NJ 08232 USA